Guynemer:
Chevalier of the Air

Guynemer:
Chevalier of the Air

Georges Guynemer, Knight of the Air
Henry Bordeaux

The Chevalier of Flight:
Captain Guynemer
Mary R. Parkman

LEONAUR

Guynemer: Chevalier of the Air
Georges Guynemer, Knight of the Air by Henry Bordeaux
The Chevalier of Flight: Captain Guynemer by Mary R. Parkman

Leonaur is an imprint of Oakpast Ltd

ISBN: 978-0-85706-723-4 (hardcover)
ISBN: 978-0-85706-724-1 (softcover)

http://www.leonaur.com

Publisher's Notes

Contents

Introduction

June 27th, 1918

My Dear M. Bordeaux:

I count the American people fortunate in reading any book of yours; I count them fortunate in reading any biography of that great hero of the air, Guynemer; and thrice over I count them fortunate to have such a book written by you on such a subject.

You, sir, have for many years been writing books peculiarly fitted to instil into your countrymen the qualities which during the last forty-eight months have made France the wonder of the world. You have written with such power and charm, with such mastery of manner and of matter, that the lessons you taught have been learned unconsciously by your readers—and this is the only way in which most readers will learn lessons at all. The value of your teachings would be as great for my countrymen as for yours. You have held up as an ideal for men and for women, that high courage which shirks no danger, when the danger is the inevitable accompaniment of duty. You have preached the essential virtues, the duty to be both brave and tender, the duty of courage for the man and courage for the woman. You have inculcated stern horror of the baseness which finds expression in refusal to perform those essential duties without which not merely the usefulness, but the very existence, of any nation will come to an end.

Under such conditions it is eminently appropriate that you should write the biography of that soldier-son of France whose splendid daring has made him stand as arch typical of the soul of the French people through these terrible four years. In this great war France has suffered more and has achieved more than any other power. To her more than to any other power, the final victory will be due. Civilization has in the past, for immemorial centuries, owed an incalculable debt to France; but for no single feat or achievement of the past does civilization owe as much to France as for what her sons and daughters have done in the world war now being waged by the free peoples against the powers of the Pit.

Modern war makes terrible demands upon those who fight. To an infinitely greater degree than ever before the outcome depends upon long preparation in advance, and upon the skilful and unified use of the nation's entire social and industrial no less than military power. The work of the general staff is infinitely more important than any work of the kind in times past. The actual machinery of both is so vast, delicate, and complicated that years are needed to complete it. At all points we see the immense need of thorough organization and of making ready far in advance of the day of trial. But this does not mean that there is any less need than before of those qualities of endurance and hardihood, of daring and resolution, which in their sum make up the stern and enduring valour which ever has been and ever will be the mark of mighty victorious armies.

The air service in particular is one of such peril that membership in it is of itself a high distinction. Physical address, high training, entire fearlessness, iron nerve, and fertile resourcefulness are needed in a combination and to a degree hitherto unparalleled in war. The ordinary air fighter is an extraordinary man; and the extraordinary air fighter stands as one in a million among his fellows. Guynemer was one of these. More than this. He was the foremost among all the extraordinary fighters of all the nations who in this war have made the skies their battle field. We are fortunate indeed in having you write his biography.

Very faithfully yours,
Theodore Roosevelt

M. Henry Bordeaux
44 Rue du Ranelagh
Paris
France

"... Guynemer Has Not Come Back"

The news flew from one air *escadrille* to another, from the aviation camps to the troops, from the advance to the rear zones of the army; and a shock of pain passed from soul to soul in that vast army, and throughout all France, as if, among so many soldiers menaced with death, this one alone should have been immortal.

History gives us examples of such universal grief, but only at the death of great leaders whose authority and importance intensified the general mourning for their loss. Thus, Troy without Hector was defenceless. When Gaston de Foix, Duke de Nemours, surnamed the Thunderbolt of Italy, died at the age of twenty-three after the victory of Ravenna, the French transalpine conquests were endangered. The bullet which struck Turenne at Saltzbach also menaced the work of Louis XIV. But Guynemer had nothing but his aeroplane, a speck in the immense spaces filled by the war. This young captain, though without an equal in the sky, conducted no battle on land. Why, then, did he alone have the power, like a great military chief, of leaving universal sadness behind him? A little child of France has given us the reason.

Among the endless expressions of the nation's mourning, this letter was written by the school-mistress of a village in Franche-Comté, Mademoiselle S—, of Bouclans, to the mother of the aviator:

Madame,
You have already received the sorrowful and grateful sympathy of official France and of France as a nation; I am venturing to send you the naïve and sincere homage of young France as represented by our school children at Bouclans. Before receiving from our chiefs the suggestion, of which

we learn today, we had already, on the 22nd of October, consecrated a day to the memory of our hero Guynemer, your glorious son.

I send you enclosed an exercise by one of my pupils chosen at random, for all of them are animated by the same sentiments. You will see how the immortal glory of your son shines even in humble villages, and that the admiration and gratitude which the children, so far away in the country, feel for our greatest aviator, will be piously and faithfully preserved in his memory. May this sincere testimony to the sentiments of childhood be of some comfort in your grief, to which I offer my most profound respect.

The Schoolmistress of Bouclans
C.S.

And this is the exercise, written by Paul Bailly, aged eleven years and ten months:

Guynemer is the Roland of our epoch: like Roland he was very brave, and like Roland he died for France. But his exploits are not a legend like those of Roland, and in telling them just as they happened we find them more beautiful than any we could imagine. To do honour to him they are going to write his name in the Pantheon among the other great names. His aeroplane has been placed in the Invalides. In our school we consecrated a day to him. This morning as soon as we reached the school we put his photograph up on the wall; for our moral lesson we learned by heart his last mention in the despatches; for our writing lesson we wrote his name, and he was the subject for our theme; and finally, we had to draw an aeroplane. We did not begin to think of him only after he was dead; before he died, in our school, every time he brought down an aeroplane we were proud and happy. But when we heard that he was dead, we were as sad as if one of our own family had died.

Roland was the example for all the knights in history. Guynemer should be the example for Frenchmen now, and each one will try to imitate him and will remember him as we have remembered Roland. I, especially, I shall never forget him, for I shall remember that he died for France, like my dear Papa.

This little French boy's description of Guynemer is true and, limited as it is, sufficient: Guynemer is the modern Roland, with the same redoubtable youth and fiery soul. He is the last of the knights-errant, the first of the new knights of the air. His short life needs only accurate telling to appear like a legend. The void he left is so great because every household had adopted him. Each one shared in his victories, and all have written his name among their own dead.

Guynemer's glory, to have so ravished the minds of children, must have been both simple and perfect, and as his biographer I cannot dream of equalling the young Paul Bailly. But I shall not take his hero from him. Guynemer's life falls naturally into the legendary rhythm, and the simple and exact truth resembles a fairy tale.

The writers of antiquity have mourned in touching accents the loss of young men cut down in the flower of their youth. "The city," sighs Pericles, "has lost its light, the year has lost its spring." Theocritus and Ovid in turn lament the short life of Adonis, whose blood was changed into flowers. And in Virgil the father of the gods, whom Pallas supplicates before facing Turnus, warns him not to confound the beauty of life with its length:

Stat sua cuique dies; breve et irreparabile tempus
Omnibus est vitae; sed famam extendere factis,
Hoc virtutis opus. . .

(The days of man are numbered, and his life-time short and irrecoverable; but to increase his renown by the quality of his acts, this is the work of virtue....)[1]

Famam extendere factis: no fabulous personage of antiquity made more haste than Guynemer to multiply the exploits that increased his glory. But the enumeration of these would not furnish a key to his life, nor explain either that secret power he possessed or the fascination he exerted.

It is not always the most brilliant actions which best expose the virtues or vices of men. Some trifle, some insignificant word or jest, often displays the character better than bloody combats, pitched battles, or the taking of cities. Also, as portrait painters try to reproduce the features and expression of their subjects, as the most obvi-

---

1: *Aeneid*, Book 10, Garnier ed.

ous presentment of their characters, and without troubling about the other parts of the body, so we may be allowed to concentrate our study upon the distinctive signs of the soul....[2]

I, then, shall especially seek out these "distinctive signs of the soul."

Guynemer's family has confided to me his letters, his notebooks of flights, and many precious stories of his childhood, his youth, and his victories. I have seen him in camps, like the Cid Campeador, who made "the swarm of singing victories fly, with wings outspread, above his tents." I have had the good fortune to see him bring down an enemy aeroplane, which fell in flames on the bank of the river Vesle. I have met him in his father's house at Compiègne, which was his Bivar. Almost immediately after his disappearance I passed two night-watches—as if we sat beside his body—with his comrades, talking of nothing but him: troubled night-watches in which we had to change our shelter, for Dunkirk and the aviation field were bombarded by moonlight. In this way I was enabled to gather much scattered evidence, which will help, perhaps, to make clear his career. But I fear—and offer my excuses for this—to disappoint professional members of the aviation corps, who will find neither technical details nor the competence of the specialist. One of his comrades of the air,—and I hope it may be one of his rivals in glory,—should give us an account of Guynemer in action. The biography which I have attempted to write seeks the soul for its object rather than the motor: and the soul, too, has its wings.

France consented to love herself in Guynemer, something which she is not always willing to do. It happens sometimes that she turns away from her own efforts and sacrifices to admire and celebrate those of others, and that she displays her own defects and wounds in a way which exaggerates them. She sometimes appears to be divided against herself; but this man, young as he was, had reconciled her to herself. She smiled at his youth and his prodigious deeds of valour. He made peace within her; and she knew this, when she had lost him, by the outbreak of her grief. As on the first day of the war, France found herself once more united; and this love sprang from her recognition in Guynemer of her own impulses, her own generous ardour, her own blood whose course has not been retarded by many long centuries.

2: Plutarch, *Life of Alexander.*

Since the outbreak of war there are few homes in France which have not been in mourning. But these fathers and mothers, these wives and children, when they read this book, will not say: "What is Guynemer to us? Nobody speaks of *our* dead." Their dead were, generally, infantry soldiers whom it was impossible for them to help, whose life they only knew by hearsay, and whose place of burial they sometimes do not know. So many obscure soldiers have never been commemorated, who gave, like Guynemer, their hearts and their lives, who lived through the worst days of misery, of mud and horror, and upon whom not the least ray of glory has ever descended! The infantry soldier is the pariah of the war, and has a right to be sensitive. The heaviest weight of suffering caused by war has fallen upon him. Nevertheless, he had adopted Guynemer, and this was not the least of the conqueror's conquests. The infantryman had not been jealous of Guynemer; he had felt his fascination, and instinctively he divined a fraternal Guynemer. When the French official dispatches reported the marvellous feats of the aviation corps, the infantry soldier smiled scornfully in his mole's-hole:

"Them again! Everlastingly them! And what about US?"

But when Guynemer added another exploit to his account, the trenches exulted, and counted over again all his feats.

He himself, from his height, looked down in the most friendly way upon these troglodytes who followed him with their eyes. One day when somebody reproached him with running useless risks in aerial acrobatic turns, he replied simply:

"After certain victories it is quite impossible not to pirouette a bit, one is so happy!"

This is the spirit of youth. "They jest and play with death as they played in school only yesterday at recreation."[3] But Guynemer immediately added:

"It gives so much pleasure to the *poilus* watching us down there."[4]

The sky-juggler was working for his brother the infantryman. As the singing lark lifts the peasant's head, bent over his furrow, so the conquering aeroplane, with its overturnings, its "loopings," its close veerings, its spirals, its tail spins, its "zooms," its dives, all its tricks of flight, amuses for a while the sad labourers in the trenches.

3: Henri Lavedan (*L'Illustration* of October 6, 1917).
4: Pierre l'Ermite (*La Croix* of October 7, 1917).

May my readers, when they have finished this little book, composed according to the rules of the boy, Paul Bailly, lift their heads and seek in the sky whither he carried, so often and so high, the tricolour of France, an invisible and immortal Guynemer!

Childhood

CHAPTER 1

The Guynemers

In his book on Chivalry, the good Léon Gautier, beginning with the knight in his cradle and wishing to surround him immediately with a supernatural atmosphere, interprets in his own fashion the sleeping baby smiling at the angels.

> According to a curious legend, the origin of which has not as yet been clearly discovered, the child during its slumber hears 'music,' the incomparable music made by the movement of the stars in their spheres. Yes, that which the most illustrious scholars have only been able to suspect the existence of is distinctly heard by these ears scarcely opened as yet, and ravishes them. A charming fable, giving to innocence more power than to proud science.[5]

The biographer of Guynemer would like to be able to say that our new knight also heard in his cradle the music of the stars, since he was to be summoned to approach them. But it can be said, at least, that during his early years he saw the shadowy train of all the heroes of French history, from Charlemagne to Napoleon.

Georges Marie Ludovic Jules Guynemer was born in Paris one Christmas Eve, December 24, 1894. He saw then, and always, the faces of three women, his mother and his two elder sisters, standing guard over his happiness. His father, an officer (Junior Class '80, Saint-Cyr), had resigned in 1890. An ardent scholar, he became a member of the Historical Society of Compiègne, and while examining the charters of the *Cartulaire de royallieu*, or writing a monograph on the *Seigneurie d'Offémont*, he verified

---

5: *La Chevalerie*, by Léon Gautier. A. Walter ed. 1895.

family documents of the genealogy of his family. Above all, it was he in reality who educated his son.

Guynemer is a very old French name. In the *Chanson de Roland* one Guinemer, uncle of Ganelon, helped Roland to mount at his departure. A Guinemer appears in *Gaydon* (the knight of the jay), which describes the sorrowful return of Charlemagne to Aix-la-Chapelle after the drama of Roncevaux; and a Guillemer figures in *Fier-à-Bras*, in which Charlemagne and the twelve peers conquer Spain. This Guillemer l'Escot is made prisoner along with Oliver, Bérart de Montdidier, Auberi de Bourgoyne, and Geoffroy l'Angevin.

In the eleventh century the family of Guynemer left Flanders for Brittany. When the French Revolution began, there were still Guynemers in Brittany,[6] but the greatgrandfather of our hero, Bernard, was living in Paris in reduced circumstances, giving lessons in law. Under the Empire he was later to be appointed President of the Tribunal at Mayence, the chief town in the country of Mont Tonnerre. Falling into disfavour after 1815, he was only President of the Tribunal of Gannat.

Here, thanks to an unusual circumstance, oral tradition takes the place of writings, charters, and puzzling trifles. One of the four sons of Bernard Guynemer, Auguste, lived to be ninety-three, retaining all his faculties. Toward the end he resembled Voltaire, not only in face, but in his irony and scepticism. He had all sorts of memories of the Revolution, the Empire, and the Restoration, of which he told extraordinary anecdotes. His longevity was owing to his having been discharged from military service at the conscription. Two of his three brothers died before maturity: one, Alphonse, infantry officer, was killed at Vilna in 1812, and the other, Jules, naval officer, died in 1802 as the result of wounds received at Trafalgar. The last son, Achille, whom we shall presently refer to again, was to perpetuate the family name.

Auguste Guynemer remembered very vividly the day when

6: There are still Guynemers there. M. Etienne Dupont, Judge in the Civil Court of Saint-Malo, sent me an extract from an *aveu collectif* of the *Leftenancy of Tinténiac de Guinemer des Rabines*. The Guynemers, in more recent times, have left traces in the county of Saint-Malo, where Mgr. Guynemer de la Hélandière inaugurated, in September, 1869, the Tour Saint-Joseph, house of the Little Sisters of the Poor in Saint-Pern.

he faced down Robespierre. He was at that time eight years old, and the mistress of his school had been arrested. He came to the school as usual and found there were no classes. Where was his teacher? he asked. At the Revolutionary Tribunal. Where was the Revolutionary Tribunal? Jestingly they told him where to find it, and he went straight to the place, entered, and asked back the captive. The audience looked at the little boy with amazement, while the judges joked and laughed at him. But without being discomposed, he explained the purpose of his visit. The incident put Robespierre in good humour, and he told the child that his teacher had not taught him anything. Immediately, as a proof of the contrary, the youngster began to recite his lessons. Robespierre was so delighted that, in the midst of general laughter, he lifted up the boy and kissed him. The prisoner was restored to him, and the school reopened.

However, of the four sons of the President of Mayence, the youngest only, Achille, was destined to preserve the family line. Born in 1792, a volunteer soldier at the age of fifteen, his military career was interrupted by the fall of the Empire. He died in Paris, in the rue Rossini, in 1866. Edmond About, who had known his son at Saverne, wrote the following biographical notice:

A child of fifteen years enlisted as a Volunteer in 1806. Junot found him intelligent, made him his secretary, and took him to Spain. The young man won his epaulettes under Colonel Hugo in 1811. He was made prisoner on the capitulation of Guadalajara in 1812, but escaped with two of his comrades whom he saved at the peril of his own life. Love, or pity, led a young Spanish girl to aid in this heroic episode, and for several days the legend threatened to become a romance. But the young soldier reappeared in 1813 at the passage of the Bidassoa, where he was promoted lieutenant in the 4th Hussars, and was given the Cross by the Emperor, who seldom awarded it. The return of the Bourbons suddenly interrupted this career, so well begun. The young cavalry officer then undertook the business of maritime insurance, earning honourably a large fortune, which he spent with truly military generosity, strewing his road with good deeds. He continued working up to the very threshold of death, for he resigned only a month ago, and it was yesterday, Thursday, that we laid him in his tomb at the age of seventy-five.

His name was Achille Guynemer. His family is related to the Benoist d'Azy, the Dupré de Saint-Maur, the Cochin, de Songis, du Trémoul and Vasselin families, who have left memories of many exemplary legal careers passed in Paris. His son, who wept yesterday as a child weeps before the tomb of such a father, is the new Sub-Prefect of Saverne, the young and laborious administrator who, from the beginning, won our gratitude and friendship.

The story of the escape from Spain contributes another page to the family traditions. The young Spanish girl had sent the prisoner a silken cord concealed in a pie. A fourth companion in captivity was unfortunately too large to pass through the vent-hole of the prison, and was shot by the English. It was August 31, 1813, after the passage of the Bidassoa, that Lieutenant Achille Guynemer was decorated with the Cross of the Legion of Honour. He was then twenty-one years of age. His great-grandson, who resembled the portraits of Achille (especially a drawing done in 1807), at least in the proud carriage of the head, was to receive the Cross at an even earlier age.

There were other epic souvenirs which awakened Georges Guynemer's curiosity in childhood. He was shown the sword and snuffbox of General Count de Songis, brother of his paternal grandmother. This sword of honour had been presented to the general by the Convention when he was merely a captain of artillery, for having saved the cannon of the fortress at Valenciennes,—though it is quite true that Dumouriez, for the same deed, wished to have him hanged. The snuffbox was given him by the Emperor for having commanded the passage of the Rhine during the Ulm campaign.

Achille Guynemer had two sons. The elder, Amédée, a graduate of the *École polytechnique*, died at the age of thirty and left no children. The second, Auguste, was sub-prefect of Saverne under the Second Empire; and, resigning this office after the war of 1870, he became Vice-President of the society for the protection of Alsatians and Lorrainers, the President of which was the Count d'Haussonville.

He had married a young Scottish lady, Miss Lyon, whose family included the Earls of Strathmore, among whose titles were those of Glamis and Cawdor mentioned by Shakespeare in *Macbeth*.

As we have already seen, only one of the four sons of the President of Mayence—the hero of the Bidassoa—had left descendants. His son is M. Paul Guynemer, former officer and historian of the *Cartulaire de Royallieu* and of the *Seigneurie d'Offémont*, whose only son was the aviator. The race whose history is lost far back in the *Chanson de Roland* and the Crusades, which settled in Flanders, and then in Brittany, but became, as soon as it left the provinces for the capital, nomadic, changing its base at will from the garrison of the officer to that of the official, seems to have narrowed and refined its stock and condensed all the power of its past, all its hopes for the future, in one last offshoot.

There are some plants, like the aloe, which bear but one flower, and sometimes only at the end of a hundred years. They prepare their sap, which has waited so long, and then from the heart of the plant issues a long straight stem, like a tree whose regular branches look like forged iron. At the top of this stem opens a marvellous flower, which is moist and seems to drop tears upon the leaves, inviting them to share its grief for the doom it awaits. When the flower is withered, the miracle is never renewed.

Guynemer is the flower of an old French family. Like so many other heroes, like so many peasants who, in this Great War, have been the wheat of the nation, his own acts have proved his nobility. But the fairy sent to preside at his birth laid in his cradle certain gilded pages of the finest history in the world: Roland, the Crusades, Brittany and Duguesclin, the Empire, and Alsace.

Chapter 2

Home and College

One of the generals best loved by the French troops, General de M——, a learned talker and charming moralist, who always seemed in his conversation to wander through the history of France, like a sorcerer in a forest, weaving and multiplying his spells, once recited to me the short prayer he had composed for grace to enable him to rear his children in the best way: "Monseigneur Saint Louis, Messire Duguesclin, Messire Bayard, help me to make my sons brave and truthful."

So was Georges Guynemer reared, in the cult of truth, and taught that to deceive is to lower oneself. Even in his infancy he was already as proud as any personage. His early years were protected by the gentle and delicate care of his mother and his two sisters, who hung adoringly over him and were fascinated by his strange black eyes. What was to become of a child whose gaze was difficult to endure, and whose health was so fragile, for when only a few months old he had almost died of infantile enteritis. His parents had been obliged to carry him hastily to Switzerland, and then to Hyères, and to keep him in an atmosphere like that of a hothouse. Petted and spoiled, tended by women, like Achilles at Scyros among the daughters of Lycomedes, would he not bear all his life the stamp of too softening an education? Too pretty and too frail, with his curls and his dainty little frock, he had an *air de princesse*. His father felt that a mistake was being made, and that this excess of tenderness must be promptly ended. He took the child on his knees; a scene as trifling as it was decisive was about to be enacted:

"I almost feel like taking you with me, where I am going."

"Where are you going, father?"

"There, where I am going, there are only men."

"I want to go with you."

The father seemed to hesitate, and then to decide:

"After all, too early is better than too late. Put on your hat. I shall take you." He took him to the hairdresser.

"I am going to have my hair cut. How do you feel about it?"

"I want to do like men."

The child was set upon a stool where, in the white combing-cloth, with his curly hair, he resembled an angel done by an Italian Primitive. For an instant the father thought himself a barbarian, and the barber hesitated, scissors in air, as before a crime. They exchanged glances; then the father stiffened and gave the order. The beautiful curls fell.

But now it became necessary to return home; and when his mother saw him, she wept.

"I am a man," the child announced, peremptorily.

He was indeed to be a man, but he was to remain for a long time also a mischievous boy—nearly, in fact, until the end.

When he was six or seven years old he began to study with the teacher of his sisters, which was convenient and agreeable, but meant the addition of another petticoat. The fineness of his feelings, his fear of having wounded any comrade, which were later to inspire him in so many touching actions, were the result of this feminine education. His walks with his father, who already gave him much attention, brought about useful reactions. Compiègne is rich in the history of the past: kings were crowned there, and kings died there. The Abbey of Saint Cornille sheltered, perhaps, the holy winding-sheet of Christ. Treaties were signed at Compiègne, and there magnificent fêtes were given by Louis XIV, Louis XV, Napoleon I, and Napoleon III. And even in 1901 the child met Czar Nicholas and Czarina Alexandra, who were staying there. So, the palace and the forest spoke to him of a past which his father could explain. And on the Place de l'Hôtel de Ville he was much interested in the bronze statue of the young girl, bearing a banner.

"Who is it?"

"Jeanne d'Arc."

Georges Guynemer's parents renounced the woman teacher, and in order to keep him near them, entered him as a day scholar at the lyceum of Compiègne. Here the child worked very little. M. Paul Guynemer, having been educated at Stanislas College, in Paris, wished his son also to go there. Georges was then twelve years old.

A journalist who had had the curiosity to investigate Georges' college days wrote in the *Journal des Débats*:

> In a photograph of the pupils of the Fifth (green) Class may be seen a restless-looking little boy, thinner and paler than the others, whose round black eyes seem to shine with a sombre brilliance. These eyes, which, eight or ten years later, were to hunt and pursue so many enemy aeroplanes, are passionately self-willed. The same temperament is evident in a snapshot of this same period, in which Georges is seen playing at war. The college registers of this year tell us that he had a clear, active, well-balanced mind, but that he was thoughtless, mischief-making, disorderly, careless; that he did not work, and was undisciplined, though without any malice; that he was very proud, and 'ambitious to attain first rank': a valuable guide in understanding the character of one who became 'the ace of aces.' In fact, at the end of the year young Guynemer received the first prize for Latin translation, the first prize for arithmetic, and four honourable mentions.

The author of the *Débats* article, who is a scholar, recalls Michelet's *mot*:

> The Frenchman is that naughty child characterized by the good mother of Duguesclin as 'the one who is always fighting the others....'

But the best portrait of Guynemer as a child I find in the unpublished notes of Abbé Chesnais, who was division prefect at Stanislas College during the four years which Guynemer passed there. The Abbé Chesnais had divined this impassioned nature, and watched it with troubled sympathy.

> His eyes vividly expressed the headstrong, fighting nature of the boy. He did not care for quiet games, but was devoted to those requiring skill, agility, and force. He had a decided preference for a game highly popular among the younger classes—*la petite guerre*. The class was divided into two ar-

mies, each commanded by a general chosen by the pupils themselves, and having officers of all ranks under his orders. Each soldier wore on his left arm a movable brassard. The object of the battle was the capture of the flag, which was set up on a wall, a tree, a column, or any place dominating the courtyard. The soldier from whom his brassard was taken was considered dead.

Guynemer, who was somewhat weak and sickly, always remained a private soldier. His comrades, appreciating the value of having a general with sufficient muscular strength to maintain his authority, never dreamed of placing him at their head. The muscle, which he lacked, was a necessity. But when a choice of soldiers had to be made, he was always counted among the best, and his name called among the first. Although he had not much strength, he had agility, cleverness, a quick eye, caution, and a talent for strategy. He played his game himself, not liking to receive any suggestions from his chiefs, intending to follow his own ideas. The battle once begun, he invariably attacked the strongest enemy and pursued those comrades who occupied the highest rank. With the marvellous suppleness of a cat, he climbed trees, flung himself to the ground, crept along barriers, slipped between the legs of his adversaries, and bounded triumphantly off with a number of brassards. It was a great joy to him to bring the trophies of his struggles to his general. With radiant face, and with his two hands resting on his legs, he looked mockingly at his adversaries who had been surprised by his cleverness. His superiority over his comrades was especially apparent in the battles they fought in the woods of Bellevue.[7] There the field was larger, and there was a greater variety of chances for surprising the enemy. He hid himself under the dead leaves, lay close to the branches of trees, and crept along brooks and ravines. It was often he who was selected to find a place of vantage for the flag. But he was never willing to act as its guardian, for he feared nothing so much as inactivity, preferring to chase his comrades through the woods. The short journey to the Bellevue woods was passed in the elaboration of various plans, and arguing about

7: The country house of Stanislas College is at Bellevue.

those of his friends; he always wanted to have the last word. The return journey was enlivened by biting criticism, which often ended in a quarrel.[8]

This is an astonishing portrait, in which nearly all the characteristics of the future Guynemer, Guynemer the fighter, are apparent. He does not care to command, he likes too well to give battle, and is already the knight of single combats. His method is personal, and he means to follow his own ideas. He attacks the strongest; neither size nor number stops him. His suppleness and skill are unequalled. He lacks the muscle for a good gymnast, and at the parallel bars, or the fixed bar, he is the despair of his instructors. How will he supply this deficiency? Simply by the power of his will. All physical games do not require physical strength, and he became an excellent shot and fencer. Furious at his own weakness, he outdid the strong, and, like Diomede and Ajax, brought back his trophies laughing. A college courtyard was not sufficient for him: he needed the Bellevue woods, while he waited to have all space, all the sky, at his disposal. So the warlike infancy of a Guynemer is like that of a Roland, a Duguesclin, a Bayard,—all are ardent hearts with indomitable energy, upright souls developing early, whose passion it was only necessary to control. The youth of Guynemer was like his childhood. As a student of higher mathematics his combative tendencies were not at all changed.

At recreation he was very fond of roller-skating, which in his case gave rise to many disputes and much pugilism. Having no respect for boys who would not play, he would skate into the midst of their group, pushing them about, seizing their arms and forcing them to waltz round and round with him like weather-cocks. Then he would be off at his highest speed, pursued by his victims. Blows were exchanged, which did not prevent him from repeating the same thing a few seconds later. At the end of recreation, with his hair disordered, his clothes covered with dust, his face and hands muddy, Guynemer was exhausted. But the strongest of his comrades could not frighten him; on the contrary, he attacked these by preference. The masters were often obliged to intervene and separate the combatants.

8: Unpublished notes by Abbé Chesnais.

Guynemer would then straighten up like a cock, his eyes sparkling and obtruding, and, unable to do more, would crush his adversary with piquant and sometimes cutting words uttered in a dry, railing voice.[9]

Talking, however, was not his forte, and his nervousness made him sputter. His speech was vibrant, trenchant, like hammer strokes, and he said things to which there was no answer. He had a horror of discussion: he was already all action.

This violence and frenzied action would have driven him to the most unreasonable and dangerous audacity if they had not been counterbalanced by his sense of honour. "He was one of those," wrote a comrade of Guynemer's, M. Jean Constantin, now lieutenant of artillery, "for whom honour is sacred, and must not be disregarded under any pretext; and in his life, in his relations with his comrades, his candour and loyalty were only equalled by his goodness. Often, in the midst of our games, some dispute arose. Where are the friends who have never had a dispute? Sometimes we were both so obstinate that we fought, but after that he was willing to renounce the privilege of the last word. He never could have endured bringing trouble upon his fellow-students. He never hesitated to admit a fault; and, what is much better, once when one of his comrades, who was a good student, had inadvertently made a foolish mistake which might have lowered his marks, I saw Georges accuse himself and take the punishment in his place. His comrade never knew anything about it, for Georges did that sort of thing almost clandestinely, and with the simplicity and modesty which were always the great charm of his character."

This sense of honour he had drawn in with his mother's milk; and his father had developed it in him. Everything about him indicated pride: the upright carriage of his head, the glance of his black eyes which seemed to pierce the objects he looked at. He loved the Stanislas uniform which his father had worn before him, and which had been worn by Gouraud and Baratier, whose fame was then increasing, and Rostand, then in all the new glory of *Cyrano* and *L'Aiglon*. He had an exact appreciation of his own dignity. Though he listened attentively in class, he would never ask for information or advice from his classmates. He hated to be trifled

9: Unpublished notes by Abbé Chesnais.

with, and made it understood that he intended to be respected. Never in all his life did he have a low thought. If he ever varied from the nobleness which was natural to him, silence was sometimes sufficient to bring him to himself.

With a mobile face, full of contrasts, he was sometimes the roguish boy who made the whole class shake with laughter, and involved it in a whirlwind of games and tricks, and at others the serious, thoughtful pupil, who was considered to be self-absorbed, distant, and not inclined to reveal himself to anybody. The fierce soldier of the *petite guerre* was also a formidable adversary at checkers. Here, however, he became patient, only moving his pieces after long reflection. None of the students could beat him, and no one could take him by surprise. If he was beaten by a professor, he never rested until he had had his revenge. His power of will was far beyond his years, but it needed to be relaxed. To study and win to the head of his class was nothing for his lively intelligence, but his health was always delicate. He would appear wrapped in cloaks, comforters, waterproof coats, and then vanish into the infirmary. This boy who did not fear blows, bruises, or falls, was compelled to avoid draughts and to diet. Nobody ever heard him complain, nor was any one ever to do so. Often he had to give up work for whole months at a time; and in his baccalaureate year he was stopped by a return of the infantile enteritis.

"Three months of rest," the doctor ordered at Christmas.

"You will do your rhetoric over again next year," said his father, who came to take him home.

"Not at all," said the boy; "the boys shall not get ahead of me"—a childish boast which passed unnoticed. At the end of three months of rest and pleasant walks around Compiègne, the child remarked: "The three months are up, and I mean to present myself in July."

"You haven't time; it is impossible." He insisted. So they discovered, at Compiègne, the Pierre d'Ailly school, in a building which since then has been ruined by a shell. It was his idea to attend these classes as a day scholar, just for the pleasure of it. He promised to continue to take care of himself at home. And in the month of July, at the age of fifteen, he took his bachelor degree, with mention.

But the bow cannot long remain bent, and hence certain diversions of his, ending sometimes in storms, but not caused by any ill-will on his part, for it was repugnant to him to give others pain. The following autumn he returned to Stanislas College, and resumed his school exploits. Again writes Abbé Chesnais:

Vexed to find that a place had been reserved for him near the professor, under the certainly justified pretext that he was too much inclined to talk, he was resolved to talk all the same, whenever he pleased. With the aid of pins, pens, wires and boxes, he soon set up a telephone which put him into communication with the boy whose desk was farthest away. He possessed tools necessary for any of his tricks, and his desk was a veritable bazaar: copybooks, books, pen-holders and paper were mixed pell-mell with the most unlikely objects, such as fragments of fencing foils, drugs, chemical products, oil, grease, bolts, skate wheels, and tablets of chocolate. In one corner, carefully concealed, were some glass tubes which awaited a favourable moment for projecting against the ceiling a ball of chewed paper. Attached to this ball, a paper personage cut out of a copybook cover danced feverishly in space. When this grotesque figurine became quiet, another paper ball, shot with great skill, renewed the dancing to the great satisfaction of the young marksman. Aeroplanes made of paper were also hidden in this desk, awaiting the propitious hour for launching them; and the professor's desk sometimes served as their landing place.... Everything, indeed, was to be found there, but in such disorder that the owner himself could never find them. Who has not seen him hunting for a missing exercise in a copybook full of scraps of paper? It is time to go to class; with his head hidden in his desk, he turns over all its contents in great haste, upsetting a badly closed ink-bottle over his books and copybooks. The master calls him to order, and he rushes out well behind all the rest of the boys.

He was not one of those ill-intentioned boys whose sole idea is to disturb the class and hinder the work of his comrades. Nor was he a ringleader. He acted entirely on his own account, and for his own satisfaction. His practical jokes never lasted long, and did not interrupt the work of others. His upright, frank and honest nature always led him to acknowledge his own acts when the master attributed them by mistake to the wrong boys. He never allowed any comrade to take his punishment for him, but he knew very well how to extricate himself from the greatest difficulties. His candour often won him some indulgence. If he happened to be punished by a timorous master, he assumed a terrible facial expression and tried to frighten him. But when, on the contrary, he found himself in the presence of a man of energy, he pleaded extenuating circumstances, and persevered until he obtained the least possible punishment. He never resented the infliction of just punishment, but suffered very much when punished in public. On the day when the class marks were read aloud, if he suspected that his own were to be bad, he took refuge in the infirmary to avoid the shame of public exposure. Honour, for him, was not a vain word.

He was very sensitive to reproaches. He was an admirer of courage, audacity, anything generous. Who at Stanislas does not remember his proud and haughty attitude when a master vexed him in presence of his classmates, or interfered to end a quarrel in which his own self-respect was at stake? All his nerves were stretched; his body stiffened, and he stood as straight as a steel rod, his arms pressed against his legs, his fists tightly closed, his head held high and rigid, and his face as yellow as ivory, with its smooth forehead, and his compressed lips cutting two deep lines around his mouth; his eyes, fixed like two black balls, seemed to start from the sockets, shooting fire. He looked as if he were about to destroy his adversary with lightning, but in reality he retained the most imperturbable sang-froid. He stood like a marble statue, but it was easy to divine the storm raging within....[10]

His tendency, after taking his bachelor's degree, was towards science; he was ambitious to enter the École polytechnique, and joined the special mathematics class. Even when very young he had shown particular aptitude for mechanics, and a gift for invention which we have seen exercised in his practical jokes as a student.

10: Unpublished notes by Abbé Chesnais.

When he was only four or five years old he constructed a bed out of paper, which he raised by means of cords and pulleys. His Stanislas classmate Lieutenant Constantin says:

> He passed whole hours in trying to solve a mathematical problem, or studying some question which had interested him, without knowing what went on around him; but as soon as he had solved his problem, or learned something new, he was satisfied and returned to the present. He was particularly interested in everything connected with the sciences. His greatest pleasure was to make experiments in physics or chemistry: he tried everything which his imagination suggested. Once he happened to produce a detonating mixture which made a formidable explosion, but nothing was broken except a few windows.

His choice of reading revealed the same tendency. He was not fond of reading, and only liked books of adventure which were food for his warlike sentiments and his ideas of honour and honesty. He preferred the works of Major Driant, and re-read them even during his mathematical year. Returning from a walk one Thursday evening, he knocked on the prefect's door to ask for a book. He wanted *La Guerre fatale*, *La Guerre de Demain*, *L'Aviateur du Pacifique*, etc. "But you have already read them."

"That does not matter."

Did he really re-read them? His dreams were always the same, and his eyes looked into the future.

Somebody, however, was to exert over this impressionable, mobile, almost too ardent nature, an influence which was to determine its direction. His father had advised him to choose his friends with care, and not yield himself to the first comer. He was not only incapable of doing that, but equally incapable of yielding himself to anybody. Do we really choose our friends in early life? We only know our friends by finding them in our lives when we need them. They are there, but we have not sought them. A similarity of taste, of sensibility, of ambitions draw us to them, and they have been our friends a long time already before we perceive that they are not merely comrades. Thus Jean Krebs became the constant companion of Georges Guynemer. The father of Jean Krebs is that Colonel Krebs whose name is connected with the first progress made in aerostation and aviation. He was then director of the Panhard factories, and his two sons were students at Stanislas. Jean, the elder, was Guynemer's classmate. He was a silent, self-centred, thoughtful student, calm in speech and facial expression, never speaking one word louder than another, and the farthest possible removed from anything noisy or agitated. Georges broke in upon his solitude and attached himself to him, while Krebs endured, smiled, and accepted, and they became allies. It was Krebs, for the time, who was the authority, the one who had prestige and wore the halo. Why, he knew what an automobile was, and one Sunday he took his friend Georges to Ivry and taught him how to drive. He taught him every technical thing he knew. Georges launched with all his energy into this new career, and soon became acquainted with every motor in existence. During the school promenades, if the column of pupils walked up or down the Champs Elysées, he told them the names of passing automobiles: "That's a Lorraine. There is a Panhard. This one has so many horsepower," etc. Woe to any who ventured to contradict him. He looked the insolent one up and down, and crushed him with a word.

He was overjoyed when the college organized Thursday afternoon visits to factories. He chose his companions in advance, sometimes compelling them to give up a game of tennis. Krebs was one of them. For Georges the visits to the Puteaux and Dion-Bouton factories were a feast of which he was often to speak later. He went, not as a sightseer, but as a connoisseur. He could not bring himself to remain with the engineer who showed the party through the works. He required more liberty, more time to investigate everything for himself, to see and touch everything. The smallest detail interested him; he questioned the workmen, asking them the use of some screw, and a thousand other things. The visit was too soon over for him; and when his comrades had already left, and the division prefect was calling the roll to make sure of all his boys, Guynemer as usual was missing, and was discovered standing in ecstasy before a machine which some workmen were engaged in setting up.

The opening weeks of the automobile and aviation exhibition were a period of comparative tranquillity for his masters, as Guynemer was no longer the same restless, nervous, mischievous boy, being too anxious to retain his privileges for the promenades. He was always one of those who haunted the prefect when the hour for departure drew near. He was impatient to know where they were to go: 'Where are we going?... Shall you take us to the Grand Palais? (The Automobile and Aviation Exhibition)....Wouldn't you be a brick!...' When they arrived, he was not one of those many curious people who circulate aimlessly around the stands with their hands in their pockets, without reaping anything but fatigue, like a cyclist on a circular track. His plans were all made in advance, and he knew where the stand was which he meant to visit. He went directly there, where his ardour and his free and easy behaviour drew upon him the admonitions of the proprietor. But nothing stopped him, and he continued to touch everything, furnishing explanations to his companions. When he returned to the college his pockets bulged with prospectuses, catalogues, and selected brochures, which he carefully added to the heterogeneous contents of his desk.[11]

Jean Krebs crystallized Georges Guynemer's vocation. He developed and specialized his taste for mechanics, separating it from vague abstractions and guiding it towards material realities and the wider experiences these procure. He deserves to be mentioned in any biography of Guynemer, and before passing on, it is proper that his premature loss should be cited and deplored. Highly esteemed as an aviator during the war, he made the best use of his substantial and reliable faculties in the work of observation. Aeroplane chasing did not attract him, but he knew how to use his eyes. He was killed in a landing accident at a time almost coincident with the disappearance of Guynemer. One of his *escadrille* mates described him thus:

> With remarkable intelligence, and a perfectly even disposition, his chiefs valued him for his sang-froid, his quick eye, his exact knowledge of the services he was able to perform. Every time a mission was entrusted to him, everybody was sure that he would accomplish it, no matter what conditions he had to meet. He often had to face enemy aeroplanes better armed than his own, and in the course of a flight had been wounded in the thigh by an exploding shell. Neverthe-

---

11: Unpublished notes by Abbé Chesnais.

less he had continued to fly, only returning considerably later when his task was done. His death has left a great void in this *escadrille*. Men like him are difficult to replace....

Thus the immoderate Guynemer had for his first friend a comrade who knew exactly his own limits. Guynemer could save Jean Krebs from his excess of literal honesty by showing him the enchantment of his own ecstasies, but Jean Krebs furnished the motor for Guynemer's ambitious young wings. Without the technical lessons of Jean Krebs, could Guynemer later have got into the aviation field at Pau, and won so easily his diploma as pilot? Would he have applied himself so closely to the study of his tools and the perfecting of his machine?

The war was to make them both aviators, and both of them fell from the sky, one in the fullness of glory, the other almost obscure. When they talked together on school outings, or as they walked along beside the walls of Stanislas, had they ever foreseen this destiny? Certainly not Jean Krebs, with his positive spirit; he only saw ahead the École polytechnique, and thought of nothing but preparation for that. But Guynemer? In his very precious notes, Abbé Chesnais shows us the boy constructing a little aeroplane of cloth, the motor of which was a bundle of elastics.

At the next recreation hour, he went up to the dormitory, opened a window, launched his machine, and presided over its evolutions above the heads of his comrades.

But these were only the games of an ingenious collegian. The worthy priest, who was division prefect, and watched the boy with a profound knowledge of psychology, never received any confidence from him regarding his vocation.

Aviation, whose first timid essays began in 1906, progressed rapidly. After Santos Dumont, who on November 22, 1906, covered 220 metres while volplaning, a group of inventors—Blériot, Delagrange, Farman, Wright—perfected light motors. In 1909 Blériot crossed the Channel, Paulhan won the height record at 1380 metres, and Farman the distance record over a course of 232 kilometres. A visionary, Viscomte Melchior de Vogué, had already foreseen the prodigious development of air-travel. All the young people of the time longed to fly. Guynemer, studying the new invention with his customary energy, could hardly do otherwise than share the general infatuation. His comrades, like himself, dreamed of parts of aeroplanes and their construction. But the idea of Lieutenant Constantin is different:

> When an aeroplane flew over the quarter, Guynemer followed it with his eyes, and continued to gaze at the sky for some time after its disappearance. His desk contained a whole collection of volumes and photographs concerning aviation. He had resolved to go up some day in an aeroplane, and as he was excessively self-willed he tried to bring this about by every means in his power. 'Don't you know anybody who could take me up some Sunday?' Of whom has he not asked this question? But at college it was not at all easy, and it was during vacation that he succeeded in carrying out his project. If I am not mistaken, his first ascension was at the aerodrome of Compiègne. At that time the comfortable cockpits of the modern aeroplanes were unknown, and the passenger was obliged to place himself as best he could behind the pilot and cling to him by putting his arms around him in order not to fall, so that it was a relief to come down again!...

The noticeable sentence in these notes is the first one: *When an aeroplane flew over the quarter, he followed it with his eyes, and continued to gaze at the sky for some time after its disappearance.*

If Jean Krebs had survived, he could perhaps enlighten us still further; but, even to this reasonable friend, could Guynemer have revealed what was still confused to himself? Jean Constantin only saw him once in a reverie; and Guynemer must have kept silent about his resolutions.

Soon afterwards, as Guynemer was obliged once more to renounce his studies—and this was the year in which he was preparing for the Polytechnique—his father left him with his grandmother in Paris, to rest. During this time he went to lectures on the social sciences, finally completing his education, which was strictly French, not one day having been passed with any foreign teacher. After this he travelled with his mother and sisters, leading the life of the well-to-do young man who has plenty of time in which to plan his future. Was he thinking of his future at all? The question occurred to his father who, worried at the thought of his son's idleness, recalled him and interrogated him as to his ideas of a future career, fully expecting to receive one of those undecided answers so often given by young men under similar circumstances. But Georges replied, as if it were the most natural thing in the world, and no other could ever have been considered:

"Aviator."

This reply was surprising. What could have led him to a determination apparently so sudden?

"That is not a career," he was told. "Aviation is still only a sport. You travel in the air as a motorist rides on the highways. And after passing a few years devoted to pleasure, you hire yourself to some constructor. No, a thousand times no!"

Then he said to his father what he had never said to anybody, and what his comrade Constantin had merely suspected:

"That is my sole passion. One morning in the courtyard at Stanislas I saw an aeroplane flying. I don't know what happened to me: I felt an emotion so profound that it was almost religious. You must believe me when I ask your permission to be an aviator."

"You don't know what an aeroplane is. You never saw one except from below."

"You are mistaken; I went up in one at Corbeaulieu."

Corbeaulieu was an aerodrome near Compiègne; and these words were spoken a very few months before the war.

* * * * * * * *

Many years before Georges Guynemer was a student at Stanislas, a professor, who was also destined to become famous, taught rhetoric there. His name was Frédéric Ozanam. He too had been a precocious child, prematurely sure of his vocation for literature. When only fifteen he had composed in Latin verse an epitaph in honour of Gaston de Foix, dead at Ravenna. This epitaph, if two words are changed—*Hispanae* into *hostilis*, and *Gaston* into *Georges*—describes perfectly the short and admirable career of Guynemer. Even the palms are included:

Fortunate heros! moriendo in saecula vives.
Eia, agite, o socii, manibus profundite flores,
Lilia per tumulum, violamque rosamque recentem
Spargite; victricis armis superaddite lauros,
Et tumulo tales mucrone inscribite voces:

Hic jacet hostilis gentis timor et decus omne
Gallorum, Georgius, conditus ante diem:
Credidit hunc Lachesis juvenem dum cerneret annos,
Sed palmas numerans credidit esse senem.[12]

It is a paraphrase of the reply of the gods to the young Pallas, in Virgil.

This young Frédéric Ozanam died in the full vigour of manhood before having attained his fortieth year, of a malady which had already foretold his death. At that time he seemed to have achieved perfect happiness; it was the supreme moment when everything succeeds, when the difficult years are almost forgotten, and the road mounts easily upward. He had in his wife a perfect companion, and his daughter was a lovable young girl. His reputation was growing; he was soon to be received by the Academy, and fortune and fame were already achieved. And then death called him. Truly the hour was badly chosen—but when is it chosen at the will of mortals? Ozanam tried to win pity from death. In his private journal he notes death's approach, concerning which he was never deceived; and he asks Heaven for a respite. To propitiate it, he offers a part of his life, the most brilliant part; he is willing to renounce honours, fame, and fortune, and will consent to live humbly and be forgotten, like the poor for whom he founded the *Conférences de Saint-Vincent de Paul,* and whom he so often visited in their wretched lodgings; but let him at least dwell a little longer in his home, that he may see his daughter grow up, and pass a few years more with the companion of his choice. Finally, he is impassioned by his Faith, he no longer reasons with Heaven, but says: "Take all according to Thy wish, take all, take myself. Thy will be done...."

Rarely has the drama of acceptance of the Divine Will been more freely developed. Now, in the drama which was to impas-

---

12:     *Fortunate hero! thou diest, but thou shalt live forever!*
        Come, my companions! strew flowers
        And lilies over the tomb! violets and young roses
        Scatter; heap up laurels upon his arms,
        And on the stone write with the point of your sword:
        Here lieth one who was the terror of the enemy, and the glory
        Of the French, George, taken before his time.
        Lachesis from his face thought him a boy,
        But counting his victories she thought him full of years.

sion Guynemer even to complete sacrifice, it is not the vocation of aviator that we should remark, but the absolute will to serve. Abbé Chesnais, who does not attach primary importance to the vocation, has understood this well. At the end of his notes he reminds us that Guynemer was a believer who accomplished his religious exercises regularly, without ostentation and without weakness.

How many times he has stopped me at night as I passed near his bed! He wanted a quiet conscience, without reproach. His usual frivolity left him at the door of the chapel. He believed in the presence of God in this holy place and respected it.... His Christian sentiments were to be a sustaining power in his aerial battles, and he would fight with the more ardour if his conscience were at peace with his God....

These words of Abbé Chesnais explain the true vocation of Guynemer:

The chances of war brought out marvellously the qualities contained in such a frail body. In the beginning did he think of becoming a pilot? Perhaps. But what he wanted above everything was to fulfil his duty as a Frenchman. He wanted to be a soldier; he was ashamed of himself, he said, in the first days of September, 1914: 'If I have to sleep in the bottom of an automobile truck, I want to go to the front. I will go.'

He was to go; but neither love of aviation nor love of fame had anything to do with his departure, as they were to have nothing to do with his final fate.

CHAPTER 3

The Departure

In the month of July, 1914, Georges Guynemer was with his family at the Villa Delphine, Biarritz, in the northern part of the Anglet beach.

This beach is blond with sunshine, but is refreshed by the ocean breezes. One can be deliciously idle there. This beach is besides an excellent landing-place for aeroplanes, because of the welcome of its soft sand. Georges Guynemer never left the Anglet beach, and every time an aeroplane descended he was there to receive it. He was the aviation sentry. But at this period aeroplanes were rare. Guynemer had his own thoughts, and tenacity was one of his dominant traits; he was already one of those who never renounce. The bathers who passed this everlasting idler never suspected that he was obstinately developing one single plan, and hanging his whole future upon it.

Meanwhile the horizon of Europe darkened. Ever since the assassination of the Archduke Ferdinand of Austria, at Sarajevo, electricity had accumulated in the air, and the storm was ready to burst. To this young man, the Archduke and the European horizon were things of nothing.

The sea-air was healthful, and he searched the heavens for invisible aeroplanes. The conversations in progress all around him were full of anxiety; he had no time to listen to them. The eyes of the women began to be full of pain; he did not notice the eyes of women. On the second of August the order for mobilization was posted. It was war!

Then Guynemer rid himself of his dream, as if it were something unreal, and broke off brusquely all his plans for the future.

He was entirely possessed by another idea, which made his eyes snap fire, and wrinkled his forehead. He rushed to his father and without taking breath announced:

"I am going to enlist."

"You are lucky."

"Well, then, you authorize me...."

"I envy you."

He had feared to be met with some parental objection on account of the uncertain health which had so often thwarted him, and had postponed his preparation for the École Polytechnique. Now he felt reassured. Next day he was at Bayonne, getting through all the necessary formalities. He was medically examined—and postponed. The doctors found him too tall, too thin—no physiological defect, but a child's body in need of being developed and strengthened. In vain he supplicated them; they were pitiless. He returned home grieved, humiliated, and furious. The Villa Delphine was to know some very uncomfortable days. His family understood his determination and began to have fears for him. And he returned to the charge, and attacked his father with insistence, as if his father were all-powerful and could, if he would, compel them to accept his son's services for *la Patrie*.

"If you would help me, I should not be put off."

"But how?"

"A former officer has connections in the army. You could speak for me."

"Very well, I will."

M. Guynemer, in his turn, went to Bayonne. From that date, indeed from the first day of war, he had promised himself never to set obstacles in the way of his son's military service, but to favour it upon all occasions. He kept his word, as we shall see later, at whatever cost to himself. The recruiting major listened to his request. It was the hour of quick enthusiasms, and he had already sustained many assaults and resisted many importunities.

"Monsieur," he now said, "you may well believe that I accept all who can serve. I speak to you as a former officer: does your conscience assure you that your son is fit to carry a knapsack and be a foot-soldier?"

"I could not say that he is."

"Would he make a cavalryman?"

"He can't ride on account of his former enteritis."

"Then you see how it is; it's proper to postpone him. Build him up, and later on he'll be taken. The war is not finished."

As Georges had been present at this interview, he now saw himself refused a second time. He returned with his father to Biarritz, pale, silent, unhappy, and altogether in such a state of anger and bitterness that his face was altered. Nothing consoled him, nothing amused him. On those magnificent August days the sea was a waste of sunshine, and the beach was an invitation to enjoy the soft summer hours; but he did not go to the beach, and he scorned the sea. His anxious parents wondered if, for the sake of his health, it would not be easier to see him depart. As for them, it was their fate to suffer in every way.

Ever since the mobilization, Georges Guynemer had had only one thought: to serve—to serve, no matter where, no matter how, no matter in what branch of the service, but to leave, to go to the front, and not stay there at Biarritz like those foreigners who had not left, or like those useless old men and children who were now all that remained of the male population.

Many trains had carried off the first recruits, trains decorated with flowers and filled with songs. The sons of France had come running from her farthest provinces, and a unanimous impulse precipitated them upon the assaulted frontier. But this impulse was perfectly controlled. The songs the men sang were serious and almost sacred. The nation was living through one of her greatest hours, and knew it. With one motion she regained her national unity, and renewed once more her youth.

Meanwhile the news that sifted in, little by little, caused intense anguish—anguish, not doubt. The government had left Paris to establish itself at Bordeaux. The capital was menaced. The enemy had entered Compiègne. Compiègne was no longer ours. The Joan of Arc on the *place* of the Hôtel de Ville had *pickelhauben* on her men-at-arms. And then the victory of the Marne lifted the weight that oppressed every heart.

At the Villa Delphine news came that Compiègne was saved. Meanwhile trains left carrying troops to reinforce the combatants. And Georges Guynemer had to live through all these departures, suffering and rebelling until he had a horror of himself. His comrades and friends were gone, or had asked permission to go. His two first cousins, his mother's nephews, Guy and René de Saint Quentin, had gone; one, a sergeant, was killed at the Battle of the Marne, the other, councillor to the Embassy at Constantinople, returning in haste when war was declared, had taken his place as lieutenant of reserves, and had been twice wounded at the Marne, by a ball in the shoulder and a shrapnel bullet in the thigh. Was it possible for him to stay there alone when the whole of France had risen?

In the *Chanson d'Aspremont*, which is one of our most captivating *chansons de geste*, Charlemagne is leaving for Italy with his army, and passes by Laon. In the donjon five children, one of whom is his nephew Roland, are imprisoned under the care of Turpin. The Emperor, who knows them well, has had them locked up for fear they would join his troops. But when they hear the ivory horns sounding and the horses neighing, they are determined to escape. They try to cajole the porter, but he is adamant and incorruptible. This faithful servitor is immediately well beaten. They take away his keys, pass over his body, and are soon out of the prison. But their adventures are only beginning. To procure themselves horses they attack and unhorse five Bretons, and to get arms they repeat the same process. They are so successful that they manage to join the Emperor's army before it has crossed the Alps. Will our new Roland allow himself to be outdistanced by these terrible children of former ages? It is not the army with its ivory horns that he has heard departing, but the whole marching nation, fighting to live and endure, and to enable honour and justice and right to live and endure with her.

So we find Guynemer once more on the Anglet beach, sad and discomfited. An aeroplane capsizes on the sand. What does he care about an aeroplane—don't they know that his old passion and dream are dead? Since August 2 he has not given them a thought. However, he begins a conversation with the pilot, who is a sergeant. And all at once a new idea takes possession of him; the old passion revives again under another form; the dream rises once more.

"How can one enlist in the aviation corps?"

"Arrange it with the captain; go to Pau."

Georges runs at once to the Villa Delphine. His parents no longer recognize the step and the face of the preceding days; he looks like their son again; he is saved.

"Father, I want to go to Pau tomorrow."

"Why this trip to Pau?"

"To enlist in the aviation corps. Before the war you wouldn't hear of my being an aviator, but in war aviation is no longer a sport."

"In war—yes, it is certainly quite another thing."

Next day he reached Pau, where Captain Bernard-Thierry was in command of the aviation camp. He forced his way through Captain Bernard-Thierry's door, over the expostulations of the sentries. He explained his case and pleaded his cause with such fire in his eyes that the officer was dazed and fascinated. From the tones of the captain's voice, when he referred to the two successive rejections, Guynemer knew he had made an impression. As he had done at Stanislas when he wanted to soften some punishment inflicted by his master, so now he brought every argument to bear, one after another; but with how much more ardour he made this plea, for his future was at stake! He bewitched his hearer. And then suddenly he became a child again, imploring and ready to cry.

"Captain, help me—employ me—employ me at anything, no matter what. Let me clean those aeroplanes over there. You are my last resource. It must be through you that I can do something at last in the war."

The captain reflected gravely. He felt the power hidden in this fragile body. He could not rebuff a suppliant like this one.

"I can take you as student mechanician."

"That's it, that's it; I understand automobiles."

Guynemer exulted, as Jean Krebs' technical lessons flashed already into his mind; they would be of great help in his work. The officer gave him a letter to the recruiting officer at Bayonne, and he went back there for the third time. This time his name was entered, he was taken, and he signed a voluntary engagement. This was on November 21, 1914. There was no need for him to explain to the family what had occurred when he returned to the Villa Delphine: he was beaming.

"You are going?" said his mother and sisters.

"Surely."

Next day he made his debut at the aviation camp at Pau as student mechanician. He had entered the army by the back door, but he had got in. The future knight of the air was now the humblest of grooms. "I do not ask any favours for him," his father wrote to the captain. "All I ask is that he may perform any services he is capable of." He had to be tried and proved deserving, to pass through all the minor ranks before being worthy to wear the *casque sacré*. The petted child of Compiègne and the Villa Delphine had the most severe of apprenticeships. He slept on the floor, and was employed in the dirtiest work about camp, cleaned cylinders and carried cans of petroleum. In this milieu he heard words and theories which dumbfounded him, not knowing then that men frequently do not mean all that they say. On November 26, he wrote Abbé Chesnais:

> I have the pleasure of informing you that after two postponements during a vain effort to enlist, I have at last succeeded. *Time and patience* ... I am writing you in the mess, while two comrades are elaborating social theories....

Would he be able to endure this workman's existence? His parents were not without anxiety. They hesitated to leave Biarritz and return to their home in Compiègne in the rue Saint-Lazare, on the edge of the forest. But, so far from being injured by manual labour, the child constantly grew stronger. In his case spirit had always triumphed over matter, and compelled it to obedience on every occasion. So now he followed his own object with indomitable energy. He took an aeroplane to pieces before mounting in it, and learned to know it in every detail.

His preparation for the École Polytechnique assured him a brilliant superiority in his present surroundings. He could explain the laws of mechanics, and tell his wonderstruck comrades what is meant by the resultant of several forces and the equilibrium of forces, giving them unexpected notions about kinematics and dynamics.[13] From the laboratory or industrial experiments then being made, he acquired, on his part, a knowledge of the resisting power of the materials used in aviation: wood, steel, steel wires, aluminium and its composites, copper, copper alloys and tissues.

13: See *Étude raisonnée de l'aéroplane*, by Jules Bordeaux, formerly student at École Polytechnique (Gauthier-Billars, edition 1912).

He saw things made—those famous wings that were one day to carry him up into the blue—with their longitudinal spars of ash or hickory, their ribs of light wood, their interior bracing of piano wire, their other bracing wires, and their wing covering. He saw the workmen prepare all the material for mortise and tenon work, saw them attach the tension wires, fit in the ends of poles, and finally connect together all the parts of an aeroplane,—wings, rudders, motor, landing frame, body. As a painter grinds his colours before making use of them, so Guynemer's prelude to his future flights was to touch with his hands—those long white hands of the rich student, now tanned and callous, often coated with soot or grease, and worthy to be the hands of a labourer—every piece, every bolt and screw of these machines which were to release him from his voluntary servitude.

One of his future comrades, *sous-lieutenant* Marcel Viallet (who one day had the honour of bringing down two German aeroplanes in ten minutes with seven bullets), thus describes him at the Pau school:

> I had already had my attention drawn to this 'little girl' dressed in a private's uniform whom one met in the camp, his hands covered with castor oil, his face all stains, his clothes torn. I do not know what he did in the workshop, but he certainly did not add to its brilliance by his appearance. We saw him all the time hanging around the 'zincs.' His highly interested little face amused us. When we landed, he watched us with such admiration and envy! He asked us endless questions and constantly wanted explanations. Without seeming to do so, he was learning. For a reply to some question about the art of flying, he would have run to the other end of the camp to get us a few drops of gasoline for our tanks....[14]

He was learning, and when he saw his way clear, he wanted to begin flying. New Year's Day arrived—that sad New Year's Day of the first year of the war. What gifts would he ask of his father? He would ask for help to win his diploma as pilot. "Don't you know somebody in your class at Saint-Cyr who could help me?"

He always associated his father with every step he took in advance. The child had no fear of creating a conflict between

---

14: *Le Petit Parisien*, September 27, 1917.

his father's love for him and the service due to France: he knew very well that he would never receive from his father any counsel against his honour, and without pity he compelled him to facilitate his son's progress toward mortal danger. Certain former classmates of M. Guynemer's at Saint-Cyr had, in fact, reached the rank of general, and the influence of one of them hastened Guynemer's promotion from student mechanician to student pilot (January 26, 1915).

On this same date, Guynemer, soldier of the 2nd Class, began his first journal of flights. The first page is as follows:

Wednesday, January 27	Doing camp chores.
Thursday, January 28	ib.
Friday, January 29	Lecture and camp chores.
Saturday, January 30	Lecture at the Blériot aerodrome.
Sunday, January 31	ib. aerodrome.
Monday, February 1	Went out twenty minutes on Blériot "roller."

The Blériot "roller," called the Penguin because of its abbreviated wings, and which did not leave the ground, was followed on Wednesday, February 17, by a three-cylinder 25 H.P. Blériot, which rose only thirty or forty metres. These were the first ascensions before launching into space. Then came a six-cylinder Blériot, and ascensions became more numerous. Finally, on Wednesday, March 10, the journal records two flights of twenty minutes each on a Blériot six-cylinder 50 H.P., one at a height of 600 metres, the other at 800, with tacking and volplaning descents. This time the child sailed into the sky. Guynemer's first flight, then, was on March 10, 1915. This journal, with its fifty pages, ends on July 28, 1916, with the following statement:

Friday, July 28.—Round at the front. Attacked a group of four enemy aeroplanes and forced down one of them. Attacked a second group of four aeroplanes, which immediately dispersed. Chased one of the aeroplanes and fired about 250 cartridges: the Boche dived, and seemed to be hit. When I shot the last cartridges from the Vickers, one blade of the screw was perforated with bullet-holes, the dislocated motor struck the machine violently and seriously injured it. Volplaned down to the aerodrome of Chipilly without accident.

A marginal note states that the aeroplane which "seemed to be hit" was brought down, and that the English staff confirmed its fall. This victory of July 28, 1916, on the Somme, was Guynemer's eleventh; and at that time he had flown altogether 348 hours, 25 minutes. This journal of fifty pages enables us to measure the distance covered.

You who in every department of achievement desire to win the trophies of a Guynemer, never forget that your progress on the path to glory begins with "doing chores."

Launched Into Space

Chapter 1

The First Victory

The apprentice pilot, then, left the ground for the first time at the Pau school on February 17, 1915, in a three-cylinder Blériot. But these were only short leaps, though sufficiently audacious ones. His monitor accused him of breakneck recklessness: "Too much confidence, madness, fantastical humour." That same evening he wrote describing his impressions to his father:

> Before departure, a bit worried; in the air, wildly amusing. When the machine slid or oscillated I was not at all troubled, it even seemed funny.... Well, it diverted me immensely, but it was lucky that *Maman* was not there.... I don't think I have achieved a reputation for prudence. I hope everything will go well; I shall soon know....

During February he made many experimental flights, and finally, on March 10, 1915, went up 600 metres. This won him next day a diploma from the Aero Club, and the day following he wrote to his sister Odette this hymn of joy—not long, but unique in his correspondence: "Uninterrupted descent, volplaning for 800 metres. Superb view (sunset)...."

"Superb view (sunset):" in the hundred and fifty or two hundred letters addressed to his family, I believe this is the only landscape. Slightly later, but infrequently, the new aviator gave a few details of observation, the accuracy of which lent them some picturesqueness; but in this letter he yielded to the intoxication of the air, he enjoyed flying as if it were his right. He experienced that sensation of lightness and freedom which accompanies the separation from earth, the pleasure of cleaving the wind, of controlling his machine, of seeing, breathing, thinking differently from the way he saw and thought and breathed on the land, of being born, in fact, into a new and solitary life in an enlarged world. As he ascended, men suddenly diminished in size. The earth looked as if some giant hand had smoothed its surface, diversified only by moving shadows, while the outlines of objects became stronger, so that they seemed to be cut in relief.

The land was marked by geometrical lines, showing man's labour and its regularity, an immense parti-coloured checker-board traversed by the lines of highroads and rivers, and containing islands which were forests and towns and cities. Was it the chain of the Pyrenees covered with snow which, breaking this uniformity, wrested a cry of admiration from the aviator? What shades of gold and purple were shed over the scene by the setting sun? His half-sentence is like a confession of love for the joy of living, violently torn from him, and the only avowal this blunt Roland would allow himself.

For the nature of his correspondence is somewhat surprising. Read superficially, it must seem extremely monotonous; but when better understood, it indicates the writer's sense of oppression, of hallucination, of being bewitched. From that moment Guynemer had only one object, and from its pursuit he never once desisted. Or, if he did desist for a brief interval, it was only to see his parents, who were part of his life, and whom he associated with his work. His correspondence with them is full of his aeroplanes, his flights, and then his enemy-chasing. His letters have no beginning and no ending, but plunge at once into action. He himself was nothing but action. Only that? the reader will ask. Action was his reason for existing, his heart, his soul—action in which his whole being fastened on his prey.

A long and minutiose training goes to the making of a good pilot. But the impatient Guynemer had patience for everything, and the self-willed Stanislas student became the hardest working of apprentices. His scientific knowledge furnished him with a method, and after his first long flights his progress was very rapid. But he wanted to master all the principles of aviation. As student mechanician he had seen aeroplanes built. He intended to make himself veritably part of the machine which should be entrusted to him. Each of his senses was to receive the education which, little by little, would make it an instrument capable of registering facts and effecting security. His eyes—those piercing eyes which were to excel in raking the heavens and perceiving the first trace of an enemy at incalculable distances—though they could only register his motion in relation to the earth and not the air, could, at all events, inform him of the slightest deviations from the horizontal in the three dimensions: namely, straightness of direction, lateral and longitudinal horizontality, and accurately appreciate angular variations. When the motor slowed up or stopped, his ear would interpret the sound made by the wind on the piano wires, the tension wires, the struts and canvas; while his touch, still more sure, would know by the degree of resistance of the controlling elements the speed action of the machine, and his skilful hands would prepare the work of death. the *Manual*, by M. Maurice Percheron, says:

> In the case of the bird its feathers connect its organs of stability with the brain; while the experienced aviator has his controlling elements which produce the movement he wishes, and inform him of the disturbing motions of the wind.

But with Guynemer the movements he wanted were never brought about as the result of reflex nervous action. At no time, even in the greatest danger, did he ever cease to govern every manoeuvre of his machine by his own thought. His rapidity of conception and decision was astounding, but was never mere instinct. As pilot, as hunter, as warrior, Guynemer invariably controlled his aeroplane and his gun with his brain. This is why his apprenticeship was so important, and why he himself attached so much importance to it—by instinct, in this case. His nerves were always strained, but he worked out his results. Behind every action was the power of his will, that power which had forced his entrance into the army, and itself closed the doors behind him, a prisoner of his own vocation.

He familiarized himself with all the levers of the engine and every part of the controlling elements. When the obligatory exercises were finished, and his comrades were resting and idling, he remounted the aeroplane, as a child gets onto his rocking-horse, and took the levers again into his hands. When he went up, he watched for the exact instant for quitting the ground and sought the easiest line of ascension; during flights, he was careful about his position, avoiding too much diving, or nosing-up, maintaining a horizontal movement, making sure of his lateral and longitudinal equilibrium, familiarizing himself with winds, and adapting his motions to every sort of rocking. When he came down, and the earth seemed to leap up at him, he noted the angle and swiftness of the descent and found the right height at which to slow down. Although his first efforts had been so clever that his monitors were convinced for a long time that he had already been a pilot, yet it is not so much his talent that we should admire as his determination. He was more successful than others because he wore himself out during the whole of his short life in trying to do better—to do better in order to serve better. He worked more than any one else; when he was not satisfied with himself he began all over again, and sought the cause of his errors. There are many other pilots as gifted as Guynemer, but he possessed an energy which was extraordinary, and in this respect excelled all the rest.

And there were no limits to the exercise of this energy. He gave his own body to complete so to speak, the aeroplane,—a centaur of the air. The wind that whistled through his tension wires and canvas made his own body vibrate like the piano wires. His body was so sensitive that it, too, seemed to obey the rudder. Nothing that concerned his voyages was either unknown or negligible to him. He verified all his instruments—the map-holder, the compass, the altimeter, the tachometer, the speedometer—with searching care. Before every flight he himself made sure that his machine was in perfect condition. When it was brought out of the hangar he looked it over as they look over race-horses, and never forgot this task. How would it be when he should have his own aeroplane?

At Pau he increased the number of his flights, and changed aeroplanes, leaving the Blériot Gnome for the Morane. His altitudes at this time varied from 500 to 600 metres. Going, on March 21, to the Avord school, he went up on the 28th to a height of 1500 metres, and on April 1 to 2600. His flights became longer, and lasted one hour, then an hour and a half. The spiral descent from a height of 500 metres, with the motor switched off, triangular voyages, the test of altitude and that of duration of flight, which were necessary for his military diploma, soon became nothing more to him than sport. In May nearly every day he piloted one passenger on an M.S.P. (Morane-Saunier-Parasol). During all this period his record-book registers only one breakdown. Finally, on May 25, he was sent to the general Aviation Reserves, and on the 31st made two flights in a Nieuport with a passenger. This was the end of his apprenticeship, and on June 8 Corporal Georges Guynemer was designated as member of Escadrille M.S.3, which he joined next day at Vauciennes.

This M.S.3 was the future N.3, the "Ciogognes" or Storks Escadrille. It was already commanded by Captain Brocard, under whose orders it was destined to become illustrious. Védrines belonged to it. *Sous-lieutenant de cavalerie* Deullin joined it almost simultaneously with Guynemer, whose friend he soon became. Later, little by little, came Heurtaux, de la Tour, Dormé, Auger, Raymond, etc., all the famous valiant knights of the escadrille, like the peers of France who followed Roland over the Spanish roads. This aviation camp was at Vauciennes, near Villers-Cotterets, in the Valois country with its beautiful forests, its chateaux, its fertile meadows, and its delicate outlines made shadowy by the humid vapour rising from ponds or woods. Guynemer wrote on June 9:

Complete calm, not one sound of any kind; one might think oneself in the Midi, except that the inhabitants have seen the beast at close range, and know how to appreciate us....Védrines is very friendly and has given me excellent advice. He has recommended me to his '*mecanos*,' who are the real type of the clever Parisian, inventive, lively and good humoured....

Next day he gives some details of his billet, and adds:

I have had a *mitrailleuse* support mounted on my machine, and now I am ready for the hunt....Yesterday at five o'clock I darted around above the house at 1700 or 2000 metres. Did you see me? I forced my motor for five minutes in hopes that you would hear me.

He had recently parted from his family, and a happy chance had brought him to fight over the very lines that protected his own home. The front of the Sixth Army to which he was attached, extending from Ribécourt beyond the forest of Laigue, passed in front of Railly and Tracy-le-Val, hollowed itself before the enemy salient of Moulin-sous-Touvent, straightened itself again near Autrèches and Nouvron-Vingré, covered Soissons, whose very outskirts were menaced, was obliged to turn back on the left bank of the Aisne where the enemy took, in January, 1915, the bridge-head at Condé, and Vailly and Chavonne, and crossed the river again at Soupir which belonged to us. Laon, La Fère, Coucy-le-Château, Chauny, Noyon, Ham, and Péronne were the objects of his reconnoitring flights.

War acts more poignantly, more directly upon a soldier whose own home is immediately behind him. If the front were pierced in the sector which had been entrusted to him, his own people would be exposed. So he becomes their sentinel. Under such conditions, *la Patrie* is no longer merely the historic soil of the French people, the sacred ground every parcel of which is responsible for all the rest, but also the beloved home of infancy, the home of parents, and, for this collegian of yesterday, the scene of charming walks and delightful vacations. He has but just now left the paternal mansion; and, not yet accustomed to the separation, he visits it by the roads of the air, the only ones which he is now free to travel. He does not take advantage of his proximity to Compiègne to go ring the familiar door-bell, because he is a soldier and respects orders; but, on returning from his rounds, he does not hesitate to turn aside a bit in order to pass over his home, indulging up there in the sky in all sorts of acrobatic caprioles to attract attention and prolong the interview. What lover was ever more ingenious and madder in his rendezvous?

Throughout all his correspondence he recalls his air visits.

You must have seen my head, for I never took my eyes off the house....

Or, after an aerial somersault that filled all those down below with terror:

I am wretched to know that my veering the other day frightened *maman* so much, but I did it so as to see the house without having to lean over the side of the machine, which is unpleasant on account of the wind....

Or sometimes he threw down a paper which was picked up in Count Foy's park:

Everything is all right.

He thought he was reassuring his parents about his safety; but their state of mind can be conceived when they beheld, exactly over their heads, an aeroplane engaged apparently in performing a dance, while through their binoculars they could see the tiny black speck of a head which looked over its side. He had indeed a singular fashion of reassuring them!

Meanwhile, at Vauciennes the newcomer was being tested. At first he was thought to look rather sickly and weak, to be somewhat reserved and distant, and too well dressed, with a "youngladyish" air. He was known to be already an expert pilot, capable of making tail spins after barely three months' experience. But still the men felt some uncertainty about this youngster whom they dared not trifle with on account of his eyes, "out of which fire and spirit flowed like a torrent."[15] Later on they were to know him better.

A legend was current as to the large quantity of "wood broken" by Guynemer in his early days with the escadrille. This is radically untrue, and his notebook contradicts it. From the very first day the *debutant* fulfilled the promise of his apprentice days. After one or two trial flights, he left for a scouting expedition on Sunday, June 13, above the enemy lines, and there met three German aeroplanes. On the 14th he described what he had seen in a letter to his father. His correspondence still included some description at that time, the earth still held his attention; but it was soon to lose interest for him:

> The appearance of Tracy and Quennevières is simply unbelievable: ruins, an inextricable entanglement of trenches almost touching one another, the soil turned over by the shells, the holes of which one sees by thousands. One wonders how there could be a single living man there. Only a few trees of a wood are left standing, the others beaten down by the *marmites*,[16] and everywhere may be seen the yellow colour of the literally ploughed-up earth. It seems incredible that all these details can be seen from a height of over 3000 metres. I could see to a distance of 60 or 70 kilometres, and never lost sight of Compiègne. Saint-Quentin, Péronne, etc., were as distinct as if I were there....

15: Saint-Simon.
16: Shells.

Next day, the 14th, another reconnaissance, of which the itinerary was Coucy, Laon, La Fère, Tergnier, Appily, Vic-sur-Aisne. Not a cannon shot disturbed these first two expeditions. But danger lurked under this apparent security, and on the 15th he was saluted by shells, dropping quite near. It was his "baptism by fire," and only inspired this sentence *à la Duguesclin*:

No impression, except satisfied curiosity.

The following days were passed in a perfect tempest, and he only laughed. The new Roland, the bold and marvellous knight, is already revealed in the letters to be given below. On the 16th he departed on his rounds, carrying, as observer, Lieutenant de Lavalette. His aeroplane was hit by a shell projectile in the right wing. On the 17th his machine returned with eight wounds, two in the right wing, four in the body, and in addition one strut and one longitudinal spar hit. On the 18th he returned from a reconnaissance with Lieutenant Colcomb during which his machine had been hit in the right wing, the rudder, and the body. But his notebook only contains statements of facts, and we have to turn to his correspondence for more details. On June 17 he wrote to his sister Odette:

Decidedly the Boches have quite a special affection for me, and the parts of my *coucou* serve me for a calendar. Yesterday we flew over Chauny, Tergnier, Laon, Coucy, Soissons. Up to Chauny my observer had counted 243 shells; Coucy shot 500 to 600; my observer estimated 1000 shots in all. All we heard was a rolling sound, and then the shells burst everywhere, below us, above, in front, behind, on the right and on the left, for we descended to take some photographs of a place which they did not want us to see. We could hear the shell-fragments whistling past; there was one that, after piercing the wing, passed within the radius of the propeller without touching it, and then to within fifty centimetres of my face; another entered by the same hole but stayed there, and I will send it to you. Fragments also struck the rudder, and one the body.

His journal mentions more:

My observer, who has been an observer from the beginning, says that he never saw a cannonade like that one, and that he was glad to get back again. At one moment a bomb-head of 105 millimetres, which we knew by its shape and the colour of its explosion, fell on us and just grazed us. In fact, we often see enormous shells exploding. It is very curious. On our return we met Captain Gerard, and my observer told him that I had astounding nerve; *zim, boum boum!* He said he knew it.... I will send you a photograph of my *coucou* with its nine bruises: it is superb.

The next day, June 18, it was his mother who received his confidences. The enemy had bombarded Villers-Cotterets with a long-distance gun which had to be discovered. On this occasion he took Lieutenant Colcomb as observer:

At Coucy, terribly accurate cannonade: *toc, toc*, two projectiles in the right wing, one within a meter of me; we went on with our observations in the same place. Suddenly a formidable crash: a shell burst 8 to 10 metres under the machine. Result: three holes, one strut and one spar spoiled. We went on for five minutes longer observing the same spot, always encircled, naturally. Returning, the shooting was less accurate. On landing, my observer congratulated me for not having moved or *zigzagged*, which would have bothered his observation. We had, in fact, only made very slight and very slow changes of altitude, speed, and direction. Compliments from him mean something, for nobody has better nerve. In the evening Captain Gerard, in command of army aviation, called me and said: 'You are a nervy pilot, all right; you won't spoil our reputation by lack of pluck—quite the contrary. For a beginner!—' and he asked me how long I had been a corporal. *Y a bon.* My *coucou* is superb, with its parts all dated in red. You can see them all, for those underneath spread up over the sides. In the air I showed each hole in the wing, as it was hit, to the passenger, and he was enchanted, too. It's a thrilling sport. It is a bore, though, when they burst over our heads, because I cannot see them, though I can hear. The observer has to give me information in that case. Just now, *le roi n'est pas mon cousin....*

Lieutenant Colcomb, has completed this account.

During the entire period of his observation, the pilot, in fact, did not make any manoeuvre or in any way shake the machine in order to dodge the firing. He simply sent the aeroplane a bit higher and calmly lowered it again over the spot to be photographed, as if he were master of the air. The following dialogue occurred:

The Observer. "I have finished; we can go back."

The Pilot: "Lieutenant, do me the favour of photographing for me the projectiles falling around us."

Children have always had a passion for pictures; and the pictures were taken.

The chasers and bombardiers in the history of aviation have attracted public attention to the detriment of their comrades, the observers, whose admirable services will become better known in time. It is by them that the battle field is exposed, and the preparations and ruses of the enemy balked: they are the eyes of the commanders, and also the friends of the troops. On April 29, 1916, Lieutenant Robbe flew over the trenches of the Mort-Homme at 200 metres, and brought back a detailed exposition of the entanglement of the lines. A year later, in nearly the same place, Lieutenant Pierre Guilland, observer on board a biplane of the Moroccan division, was forced down by three enemy aeroplanes just at the moment when his division, whose progress he was following in order to report it, started its attack on the Corbeaux Woods east of the Mort-Homme, on August 20, 1917. He fell on the first advancing lines and was picked up, unconscious and mortally wounded, by an artillery officer who proceeded to carry out the aviator's mission. When the latter reopened his eyes—for only a short while—he asked:

"Where am I?"

"North of Chattancourt, west of Cumières."

"Has the attack succeeded?"

"Every object has been attained."

"Ah! that's good, that's good." ... He made them repeat the news to him. He was dying, but his division was victorious.

Near Frise, Lieutenant Sains, who had been obliged to land on July 1, 1916, was rescued by the French army on July

4, after having hidden himself for three days in a shell-hole to avoid surrendering, his pilot, Quartermaster de Kyspotter, having been killed.

During the battle of the Aisne in April, 1917, Lieutenant Godillot, whose pilot had also been killed, slid along the plane, sat on the knees of the dead pilot, and brought the machine back into the French lines. And Captain Méry, Lieutenant Viguier, Lieutenant de Saint-Séverin, and Fressagues, Floret, de Niort, and Major Challe, Lieutenant Boudereau, Captain Roeckel, and Adjutant Fonck—who was to become famous as a chaser—how many of these elite observers furthered the destruction wrought by the artillery, and aided the progress of the infantry!

On October 24, 1916, as the fog cleared away, I saw the aeroplane of the Guyot de Salins division fly over Fort Douaumont just at the moment when Major Nicolai's marines entered there.[17] The aeroplane had descended so low into the mist that it seemed as if magnetically drawn down by the earth, and the observer, leaning over the edge, was clapping his hands to applaud the triumph of his comrades. The latter saw his gesture, even though they could not hear the applause, and cheered him—a spontaneous exchange of soldierly confidence and affection between the sky and the earth.

Almost exactly one year later, on October 23, 1917, I saw the aeroplane of the same division hovering over the Fort of the Malmaison just as the Giraud battalion of the 4th Zouaves Regiment took possession of it. At dawn it came to observe and note the site of the commanding officer's post, and to read the optical signals announcing our success. At each visit it seemed like the moving star of old, now guiding the new shepherds, the guardians of our dear human flocks—not over the stable where a God was born, but over the ruins where victory was born.

* * * * * * * *

Later on Captain Colcomb spoke of Guynemer as "the most sublime military figure I have ever been permitted to behold, one of the finest and most generous souls I have ever known." Guyne-

---

17: See *Les Captifs délivrés.*

THE FIRST FLIGHT IN A BLÉRIOT

mer was not satisfied to be merely calm and systematically immovable, and to display sang-froid, though to an extraordinary degree. He amused himself by counting the holes in his wings, and pointing them out to the observer. He was furious when the explosions occurred outside his range of vision, because he was not resigned to missing anything. He seemed to juggle with the shrapnel. And after landing, he rushed off to his escadrille chief, Captain Brocard, took him by the arm, and never left him until he had drawn him almost by force to his machine, compelling him to put his fingers into the wounds, exulting meanwhile and fairly bounding with joy. Captain Brocard, felt quite sure of him from that time, and referred to him later in these words:

Very young: his extraordinary self-confidence and natural qualities will very soon make him an excellent pilot....

His curiosity, indeed, was satisfied; and to whom would he confide all the risks that he ran? His mother and his sisters, the hearts which were the most troubled about him, and whose peace and happiness he had carried off into the air. He never dreamed of the torment he caused them, and which they knew how to conceal from him. Even the idea of such a thing never occurred to him. As they loved him, they loved him just as he was, in the raw. He was too young to dissimulate, too young to spare them. He knew nothing either of lies or of pity. He never thought that any one could suffer anguish about a son or a brother when this son and brother was himself supremely happy in his vocation. He was naïvely cruel.

But the rounds and reconnaissances were not to hold him long; and he already scented other adventures. He had scented the odour of the beast, and he had his aeroplane furnished with a support for a machine-gun. That particular aeroplane, it is true, came to an untimely end in a ditch, but was already condemned by its body-frame, which was rotten with bullet holes. That was the only "wood" Guynemer "broke" during his early flights.

But his next aeroplane was also armed, and in the young pilot could already be plainly seen that taste for enemy-chasing which was to bewitch and take possession of him. Though after this time he certainly carried over the lines Lieutenant de Lavalette, Lieutenant Colcomb and Captain Siméon, and always with equal calm, yet he aspired to other flights, further away from earth. Lieutenant de Beauchamp—the future Captain de Beauchamp, who was to die so soon after his audacious raids on Essen and Munich—divined what was hidden in this thin boy who was in such breathless haste to get on. He would not allow Corporal Guynemer to address him as lieutenant, feeling so surely his equality, and tomorrow perhaps his mastery. On July 6, 1915, he sent him a little guide for aviators in a few lines:

Be cautious. Look well at what is happening around you before acting. Invoke Saint Benoît every morning. But above all, write in letters of fire in your memory: *In aviation, everything not useful should be avoided.*

Oh, of course! The "little girl" laughed at the advice as he laughed at the tempest. He had an admiration for Beauchamp, but when did a Roland ever listen to an Oliver? One day he went up in a wind of over 25 metres, and even by nosing-up a bit he could hardly make any progress. With the wind behind him he made over 200 kilometres. Then he landed. Védrines addressed a few warning remarks to him, and he was thought to be calmed. But off he went again before the frightened spectators. He would always do too much, and nothing could restrain him.

The importance of the development of aviation in the war had been foreseen neither by the Germans nor ourselves. If before the beginning of the campaign the military chiefs had understood all the services which would be rendered by aerial strategic scouting, the regulation of artillery fire would not have still been in an experimental stage. No one knew the help which was to be derived from aerial photography. The air duel was regarded simply as a possible incident that might occur during a patrol or a reconnaissance, and in view of which the observer or mechanician armed himself with a gun or an automatic pistol. Aeroplanes armed with machine-guns were very exceptional, and at the end of 1914 there were only thirty. The Germans used them generally before we did; but it was the French aviators, nevertheless, who forced the Germans to fight in the air. I had the opportunity in October, 1914, to see, from a hill on the Aisne, one of these first aeroplane combats, which ended by the enemy falling on the outskirts of the village of Muizon on the left bank of the Vesle. The French champion bore the fine name of Franc, and piloted a Voisin. At that date it was not unusual to pick up messages dropped within our lines by enemy pilots, substantially to this effect:

Useless for us to fight each other; there are enough risks without that....

Meanwhile, strategic reconnaissance was perfected as the line of the front became firmly established, and more and more importance was accorded to the search for objectives. Remarkable results were attained by air photography from December, 1914; and after January, 1915, the regulation of artillery fire by wireless telegraphy was in general practice. It was necessary to protect the aeroplanes attached to army corps, and to clean up the air for their free circulation. This role devolved upon the most rapid aeroplanes, which were then the Morane-Saunier-Parasols, and in the spring of 1915 these formed the first *escadrilles de chasse*, one for each army. Garros, already popular before the war for having been the first air-pilot to cross the Mediterranean, from Saint-Raphael to Bizerto, forced down a large Aviatik above Dixmude in April, 1915. A few days later a motor breakdown compelled him to land at Ingelminster, north of Courtrai, and he was made prisoner.[18] The aviators, like the knights of ancient times, sent one another challenges. Sergeant David—who was killed shortly after—having been obliged to refuse to fight an enemy aeroplane because his machine-gun jammed, dropped a challenge to the latter on the German aerodrome, and waited at the place, on the day and hour fixed, at Vauquois (noon, in June, 1915, above the German lines), but his adversary never came to the rendezvous.

The Maurice Farman and Caudron aeroplanes were used for observation. The Voisin machines, strong but slower, were more especially utilized for bombardments, which began to be carried out by organized expeditions. The famous raids on the Ludwigshafen factories and the Karlsruhe railway station occurred in June, 1915. It was at the battle of Artois (May and June, 1915) that aviation for the first time constituted a branch of the army; and the work was chiefly done by the escadrilles belonging to the army corps, which rendered very considerable services as scouts and in aerial

18: The romantic circumstances under which he escaped in February, 1918, are well known.

photography and destructive fire. But as an enemy chaser, the aeroplane was still regarded with much distrust and incredulity. Some said it was useless; was it not sufficient that the aeroplanes of the army corps and those for bombardments could defend themselves? Others of less extreme opinions thought it should be limited to the part of protector. This opposition was overcome by the sudden development of the German enemy-chasing aeroplanes after July, 1915, subsequent to our raids on Ludwigshafen and Karlsruhe, which aroused furious anger in Germany.

In the beginning the belligerent nations had collected the most heterogeneous group of all the aeroplane models then available. But the methodical Germans, without delay, supplied their constructors with definite types of machines in order to make their escadrilles harmonious. At that time they used monoplanes for reconnaissances, without any special arrangement for carrying arms, and incapable of carrying heavy weights; and biplanes for observation, unarmed, and possessing only a makeshift contrivance for launching bombs. The machines of both these series were two-seated, with the passenger in front. These were Albatros, Aviatiks, Eulers, Rumplers, and Gothas. Early in 1915 appeared the Fokkers, which were one-seated, and new two-seated machines, Aviatiks or Albatros, which were more rapid, with the passenger at the rear, and furnished with a revolving turret for the machine-gun. The German troops engaged in aerostation, aviation, automobile and railway service were grouped as communication troops (*Verkehrstruppen*), under the direction of the General Inspection of Military Communications. It was not until the autumn of 1916 that the aerostation, aviation, and aerial defence troops were made independent and, under the title of *Luftstreitkräfte* (aerial combatant forces), took their position in the order of battle between the pioneers and the communication troops. But early in the summer of 1915 the progress realized in aviation resulted in its forming a separate branch of the army, with campaign and enemy-chasing escadrilles.

Guynemer was now on the straight road toward aerial combat. Most of our pilots were still chasing enemy aeroplanes with one passenger armed with a simple musketoon. More circumspect than the others, Guynemer had his aeroplane armed with a machine-gun. Meanwhile the staff was preparing to reorganize the army escadrilles.

The bold Pégoud had several times fought with too enterprising Fokkers or Aviatiks; Captain Brocard had forced down one of them in flames over Soissons; and the latest recruit of the escadrille, this youngster of a Guynemer, was burning to have his own Boche.

The first entries in his notebook of flights for July, 1915, record expeditions without result, in company with Adjutant Hatin, Lieutenant de Ruppiere, in the region of Noyon, Roye, Ham, and Coucy-le-Château. On the 10th, the *chasseurs* put to flight three Albatros, while a more rapid Fokker attempted an attack, but turned back having tried a shot at their machine-gun. On the 16th Guynemer and Hatin dropped bombs on the Chauny railway station; during the bombardment an Aviatik attacked them, they stood his fire, replying as well as they could with their musketoon, and returned to camp uninjured. Adjutant Hatin was decorated with the Military Medal. As Hatin was a *gourmet*, Guynemer went that same evening to Le Bourget to fetch two bottles of Rhine wine to celebrate this family fête. At Le Bourget he tried the new Nieuport machine, which was the hope of the fighting aeroplanes. Finally, on July 19—memorable date—his journal records Guynemer's first victory:

> Started with Guerder after a Boche reported at Couvres and caught up with him over Pierrefonds. Shot one belt, machine-gun jammed, then unjammed. The Boche fled and landed in the direction of Laon. At Coucy we turned back and saw an Aviatik going toward Soissons at about 3200 metres up. We followed him, and as soon as he was within our lines we dived and placed ourselves about 50 metres under and behind him at the left. At our first salvo, the Aviatik lurched, and we saw a part of the machine crack. He replied with a rifle shot, one ball hitting a wing, another grazing Guerder's hand and head. At our last shot the pilot sank down on the body-frame, the observer raised his arms, and the Aviatik fell straight downward in flames, between the trenches....

This flight began at 3700 metres in the air, and lasted ten minutes, the two combatants being separated by a distance of 50 and sometimes 20 metres. The statement of fact is characteristic of Guynemer. An unforgettable sight had been imprinted on his eyes: the pilot sinking down in his cock-pit, the arms of the observer beating the air, the burning aeroplane sinking. Such were to be his future landscape sketches, done in the sky. The wings of the bird of prey were unfurled definitely in space.

The two fighting airmen had left Vauciennes at two o'clock in the afternoon, and at quarter-past three they landed, conquerors, at Carrière l'Evêque. From their opposing camps the infantry had followed the fight with their eyes. The Germans, made furious by defeat, cannonaded the landing-place. Georges, who was too thin for his clothes, and whose leather pantaloons lined with sheepskin, which he wore over his breeches, slipped and impeded his walking, sat down under the exploding shells and calmly took them off. Then he placed the machine in a position of greater safety, but broke the propeller on a pile of hay. During this time a crowd had come running and now surrounded the victors. Artillery officers escorted them off, sentinels saluted them, a colonel offered them champagne. Guerder was taken first into the commanding officer's post, and on being questioned about the manoeuvre that won the victory excused himself with modesty:

"That was the pilot's affair."

Guynemer, who had stolen in, was willing to talk.

"Who is this?" asked the colonel.

"That's the pilot."

"You? How old are you?"

"Twenty."

"And the gunner?"

"Twenty-two."

"The deuce! There are nothing but children left to do the fighting."

So, passed along in this manner from staff to staff, they finally landed at Compiègne, conducted by Captain Siméon. No happiness was complete for Guynemer if his home was not associated with it.

"He will get the Military Medal," declared Captain Siméon, "because he wanted his Boche and went after him."

Words of a true chief who knew his men. Always to go after what he wanted was the basic characteristic of Guynemer. And now various details concerning the combat came one by one to light. Guerder had been half out of the machine to have the machine-gun ready to hand. When the gun jammed, Georges yelled to his comrade how to release it. Guerder, who had picked up his rifle, laid it down, executed the manoeuvre indicated by Guynemer, and resumed his machine-gun fire. This episode lasted two minutes during which Georges maintained the aeroplane under the Aviatik, unwilling to change his position, as he saw that a recoil would expose them to the Boche's gun.

Meanwhile Védrines came in search of the victor, and piloted the machine back to head-quarters, with Guynemer on board seated on the body and quivering with joy.

With this very first victory Guynemer sealed his friendship with the infantry, whom his youthful audacity had comforted in their trenches. He received the following letter, dated July 20, 1915:

Lieutenant-Colonel Maillard
Commanding the 238th Infantry

To Corporal Pilot Guynemer and Mechanician Guerder
Escadrille M.S. 3, at Vauciennes

The lieutenant-colonel
The officers
The whole regiment,
Having witnessed the aerial attack you made upon a German Aviatik over their trenches, spontaneously applauded your victory which terminated in the vertical fall of your adversary. They offer you their warmest congratulations, and share the joy you must have felt in achieving so brilliant a success.
Maillard

On July 21 the Military Medal was given to the two victors, Guynemer's being accompanied by the following mention:

Corporal Guynemer: a pilot full of spirit and audacity, volunteering for the most dangerous missions. After a hot pursuit, gave battle to a German aeroplane, which ended in the burning and destruction of the latter.

The decoration was bestowed on August 4 at Vauciennes by General Dubois, then in command of the Sixth Army, and in presence of his father, who had been sent for. Then Guynemer paid for his newly won glory by a few days of fever.

CHAPTER 2

From the Aisne to Verdun

Guynemer's first victory occurred on July 19, 1915, and for his second he had to wait nearly six months. This was not because he had not been on the watch. He would have been glad to mount a Nieuport, but, after all, he had had his Boche, and at that time the exploit was exceptional: he had to be patient, and give his comrades a chance to do the same.

When finally he obtained the longed-for Nieuport, he flew sixteen hours in five days, and naturally went to parade himself over Compiègne. Without this dedication to his home, the machine would never be consecrated.

When the overwork incident to such a life forced him to take a little repose, he wandered back to his home like a soul in pain. It was in vain that his parents and his two sisters—whom he called his "kids" as if he were their elder—exhausted their ingenuity to amuse him. This home he loved so much, which he left so recently, and returned to so happily, bringing with him his young fame, no longer sufficed him. Though he was so comfortable there, yet on clear days the house stifled him. On such days he seemed like a school child caught in some fault: a little more and he would have condemned himself. Then his sister Yvonne, who had understood the situation, made a bargain with him.

"What is it you miss here at home?"

"Something you cannot give me. Or rather, yes, you can give it to me. Promise me you will."

"Surely, if it will make you happy."

"I shall be the happiest of men."

"Then it's granted in advance."

"Very well, this is it: every morning you must examine the weather. If it is bad, you will let me sleep."

"And if it is fine?"

"If it is fine, you will wake me up."

His sister was afraid to ask more, as she guessed how he would use a fine day. As she was silent, he pretended to pout with that cajoling manner he could assume, and which fascinated everybody.

"You won't do it? I could not stay home: *c'est plus fort que moi.*"

"But, I promise."

And to keep him at home until he should be cured, more or less, the young girl opened her window every morning and inspected the sky, secretly hoping to find it thickly covered with clouds.

"Clouds, waiting over there, motionless, on the edge of the horizon, what are you waiting for? Will you stand idle and let me awaken my brother, who is resting?"

The clouds being indifferent, the sleeper had to be awakened. He dressed hastily, with a smile at the transparent sky, and soon reached Vauciennes by automobile, where he called for his machine, mounted, ascended, flew, hunted the enemy, and returned to Compiègne for luncheon.

"And you can leave us like that?" remonstrated his mother. "Why, this is your holiday."

"Yes, the effort to leave is all the greater."

"Well?—"

"I like the effort, *Maman.*"

His Antigone forced herself to keep her bargain with him. The sun never shone above the forest in vain, but nevertheless she detested the sun. What a strange Romeo this boy would have made! Without the least doubt he would have charged Juliet to wake him to go to battle, and would never have forgiven her for confounding the lark and the nightingale. On his return to the aviation camp, in the absence of his own longed-for victories, he took pleasure in describing those of others. He knew nothing of rivalry or envy. He wrote his sister Odette the following description of a combat waged by Captain Brocard, who surprised a Boche from the rear, approached him to within fifteen metres without being seen, and, just at the moment when the enemy pilot turned round his head, sent him seven cartridges from his machine-gun:

Result: one ball in the ear, and another through the middle of his chest. You can imagine whether the fall of the machine was instantaneous or not. There was nothing left of the pilot but one chin, one ear, one mouth, a torso and material enough to reconstitute two arms. As to the *coucou* (burned), nothing was left but the motor and a few bits of iron. The passenger was emptied out during the fall....

It cannot be said that he had much consideration for the nerves of young girls. He treated them as if they were warriors who could understand everything relating to battles. He wrote with the same freedom that Shakespeare's characters use in speech.

Until the middle of September he piloted two-seated aeroplanes, carrying one passenger, either as observer or combatant. At last he went up in his one-seated Nieuport, revelling in the intoxication of being alone, that intoxication well known to lovers of the mountains and the air. Is it the sensation of liberty, the freedom from all the usual material bonds, the feeling of coming into possession of these deserts of space or ice where the traveller covers leagues without meeting anybody, the forgetfulness of all that interferes with one's own personal object? Such solitaries do not easily accommodate themselves to company which seems to them to encroach upon their domain, and steal a part of their enjoyment. Guynemer never enjoyed anything so much as these lonely rounds in which he took possession of the whole sky, and woe to the enemy who ventured into this immensity, which was now his park.

On September 29, and October 1, 1915, he was sent on special missions. These special missions were generally confided to Védrines, who had accomplished seven. The time is not yet ripe for a revelation of their details, but they were particularly dangerous, for it was necessary to land in occupied territory and return. Guynemer's first mission required three hours' flying. He ascended in a storm, just as the countermand arrived owing to the unfavourable weather. When he descended, volplaning, at daybreak, with slackened, noiseless motor, and landed on our invaded territory, his heart beat fast. Some peasants going to their work in the fields saw him as he ascended again, and recognizing the tricolour, showed much surprise, and then extended their hands to him. This mission won for Sergeant Guynemer—he had been promoted sergeant shortly before—his second mention:

> Has proved his courage, energy and sang-froid by accomplishing, as a volunteer, an important and difficult special mission in stormy weather.

"This palm is worth while," he wrote in a letter to his parents, "for the mission was hard." On his way back an English aviator shot at him, but on recognizing him signalled elaborate excuses.

Some rather exciting reconnaissances with Captain Siméon—one day over Saint-Quentin they were attacked by a Fokker and, their machine-gun refusing to work, they were subjected to two hundred shots from the enemy at 100 metres, then at 50 metres, so that they were obliged to dive into a cloud, with one tyre gone—and a few bombardments of railway stations and goods depots did not assuage his fever for the chase. Nothing sufficed him but to explore and rake the heavens. On November 6, 3000 metres above Chaulnes, he waged an epic combat with an L.V.G. (*Luft-Verkehr-Gesellschaft*), 150 H.P. Having succeeded in placing himself three metres under his enemy, he almost laughed with the surety he felt of forcing him down, when his machine-gun jammed. He immediately banked, but he was so near the enemy that the machines interlocked. Would he fall? A bit of his canvas was torn off, but the aeroplane held its own. As he drew away he saw the enormous enemy machine-gun aimed at him. A bullet grazed his head. He dived under the Boche, who retreated. "All the same," Guynemer added gaily, "if I ever get into a terrible financial fix and have to become a cab-driver, I shall have memories which are far from ordinary: a tyre exploding at 3400 metres, an interlocking at 3000 metres. That rotten Boche only owed his life to a spring being slightly out of order, as was shown by the autopsy on the machine-gun. For my eighth combat, this was decidedly annoying...."

It was annoying, but what could be done? Nothing, in fact, but return to one's apprenticeship. He was perfectly satisfied with his work as a pilot, but it was necessary to avoid these too frequent jammings which saved the enemy. At Stanislas College Guynemer was known as an excellent shot. He began to practice again with his rifle, and with the machine-gun; above all, he carefully examined every part of this delicate weapon, taking it apart and putting it together, and increasing his practice. He became a gun-smith. And there lies the secret of his genius: he never gave up anything, nor ever acknowledged himself beaten. If he failed, he began all over again, but after having sought the cause of his failure in order to remedy it. When he was asked one day to choose a device for himself, he adopted this, which completely expresses his character: *Faire face*. He always faced everything, not only the enemy, but every object which opposed his progress. His determination compelled success. In the career of Guynemer nothing was left to chance, and everything won by effort, pursuit, and implacable will. On Sunday, December 5, 1915, as he was making his rounds in the Compiègne region, he saw two aeroplanes more than 3000 metres above Chauny. As the higher one flew over Bailly he sprang upon it and attacked it: at 50 metres, fifteen shots from his machine-gun; at 20 metres, thirty shots. The German fell in a tail spin, north of Bailly over against the Bois Carré. Guynemer was sure he had forced him down; but the other aeroplane was still there. He tacked in order to chase and attack him, but in vain, for his second adversary had fled. And when he tried to discover the spot where the first must have fallen, he failed to find it. This was really too much: was he going to lose his prey? Suddenly he had an idea. He landed in a field near Compiègne. It was Sunday, and just noon, and he knew that his parents would be coming home from mass. He watched for them, and as soon as he perceived his father rushed to him:

"Father, I have lost my Boche."

"You have lost your Boche?"

"Yes, an aeroplane that I have forced down. I must return to my escadrille, but I don't want to lose him."

"What can I do?"

"Why, look for him and find him. He ought to be near Bailly, towards the Bois Carré."

And he vanished, leaving to his father the task of finding the lost aeroplane as a partridge is found in a field of lucerne. The military authority kindly lent its aid, and in fact the body of the German pilot was discovered on the edge of the Bois Carré, where it was buried.

This victory was ratified, but a few days later the authorities, failing to find the necessary material proof, refused to give Guynemer credit for it. Ah, the regulations refuse the hunter this game? Guynemer, turning very red, declared: "It doesn't matter, I will get another."

He was always wanting another; and in fact he got one four days later, on December 8. This is the report in his notebook:

> Discovering the strategic line Royne-Nesle. While descending, saw a German aeroplane high, and far within its own lines. As it passed the lines at Beuvraigne, I cut off its retreat and chased it. I caught up to it in five minutes, and fired forty-seven shots from my Lewis from a point 20 metres behind and under it. The enemy aeroplane, an L.V.G. 165 H.P. probably, dived, caught fire, turned over, and, carried along by the west wind, fell on its back at Beuvraigne. The passenger fell out at Bus, the pilot at Tilloloy....

When the victor landed at Beuvraigne near his victim, the artillerymen belonging to a nearby battery of 95 mm. guns (47th battery of the 31st regiment of artillery), and who were already crowding around the enemy's body, rushed upon and surrounded Guynemer. But the commander, Captain Allain Launay, mustered his men, ordered a salute to Guynemer, made a speech to his command, and said: "We shall now fire a volley in honour of Sergeant Guynemer."

The salvo demolished a small house where some Boches had taken refuge. Through the binoculars they could be seen to scatter when the first shell struck their shelter.

"They owe that to me, too!" cried the enthusiastic urchin.

Meanwhile Captain Allain Launay had patiently ripped the captain's stripes from his cap, and when he had finished handed them to Guynemer:

"Promise me to wear them when you are appointed captain."

This victory was not questioned, and there was even some discussion about making this youngster a Knight of the Legion of Honour. But even when he had been promoted sergeant there had been some objection, owing to his youth.

"Nevertheless," Guynemer had observed angrily, "I am not too young to be hit by the enemy's shells."

This time another objection arose: If he receives the "cross" for this victory, what can be given him for succeeding ones? The proud little Roland rebelled, revolted, rose up like a cock on its spurs. He did not see that everybody already foresaw his destiny. He would have his "cross," he would have it, and he would not wait long for it, either. He would know how to wring it out of them.

Six days later, December 14, with his comrade, the sober and calm Bucquet, he attacked two Fokkers, one of which was dashed to pieces in its fall, while the other damaged his own machine. A letter to his father described the combat in his own brief and direct manner, without a superfluous word:

> Combat with two Fokkers. The first, trapped, and his passenger killed, dived upon me without having seen me. Result: 35 bullets at close quarters and *couic*! The fall was seen by four other aeroplanes (3 plus 1 makes 4, and perhaps that will win me the 'cross'). Then combat with the second Fokker, a one-seated machine shooting through the propeller, as rapid and easily handled as mine. We fought at ten metres, both turning vertically to try to get behind.
>
> My spring was slack: compelled to shoot with one hand above my head, I was handicapped; I was able to shoot twenty-one times in ten seconds. Once we almost telescoped, and I jumped over him—his head must have passed within fifty centimetres of my wheels. That disgusted him; he went away and let me go. I came back with an intake pipe burst, one rocker torn away: the splinters had made a number of holes in my over-coat and two notches in the propeller. There were three more in one wheel, in the body-frame (injuring a cable), and in the rudder.

All these accounts of the chase, cruel and clear, seem to breathe a savage joy and the pride of triumph. The sight of a burning aeroplane, of an enemy sinking down, intoxicated him. Even the remains of his enemies were dear to him, like treasures won by his young strength. The shoulder-straps and decorations worn by his adversary who fell at Tilloloy were given over to him; and Achilles before the trophies of Hector was not more arrogant. These combats in the sky, more than nine thousand feet above the earth, in which the two antagonists are isolated in a duel to the death, scarcely to be seen from the land, alone in empty space, in which every second lost, every shot lost, may cause defeat—and what a defeat! falling, burning, into the abyss beneath—in which they fight sometimes so near together, with short, unsteady thrusts, that they see each other like knights in the lists, while the machines graze and clash together like shields, so that fragments of them fall down like the feathers of birds of prey fighting beak to beak—these combats which require the simultaneous handling of the controlling elements and of the machine-gun, and in which speed is a weapon, why should they not change these young men, these children, into demigods? Hercules, Achilles, Roland, the Cid—where shall we find outside of mythology or the epics any prototypes for the wild and furious Guynemer?

On the day of his coming of age, December 24, 1915—earlier than his ancestor under the Empire—he received the Cross of the Legion of Honour, with this mention:

> Pilot of great value, model of devotion and courage. Has fulfilled in the past six months two special missions requiring the finest spirit of sacrifice, and has waged thirteen aerial combats, two of which ended in the enemy aeroplanes falling in flames.

This mention was already out of date, having been based upon the report dated December 8. To the two victories therein mentioned should be added those of the 5th and the 14th of December. Decorated at the age of twenty-one, the enlisted mechanician of Pau continued to progress at breakneck speed. The red ribbon, the yellow ribbon and green War Medal with four palms, are very becoming to a young man's black coat. Georges Guynemer never despised these baubles, nor in any way concealed the pleasure they afforded him. He knew how high one has to climb to pick them. And he was eager for more and more, not because of vanity, but for what they signified.

On the 3rd and 5th of February, 1916, new combats took place, always in the region of Roy and Chaulnes. On February 3 he met three enemies within forty minutes, on the same round:

> Attacked at 11.10 an L.V.G., which replied with its machine-gun. Fired 47 shots at 100 metres; the enemy aeroplane dived swiftly down to its own lines, smoking. Lost to view at 500 metres from the ground. At 11.40 attacked

an L.V.G. (with Parabellum) from behind, at 20 metres; it tacked and dived spirally, pursued neck to neck at 1300 metres. It fell three kilometres from its lines. I rose again and lost sight of it. (This aeroplane had wings of the usual yellow colour, its body was blue like the N., and its outlines seemed similar to that of the *monococques*.) At 11.50 attacked an L.V.G., which immediately dived into the clouds and disappeared. Landed at Amiens.

He cleared the sky of every Boche: one fallen and two put to flight is not a bad record. He always attacked. With his accurate eyes he tracked out the enemy in the mystery of space, and placing himself higher, tried to surprise him. On the 5th, near Frise, he closed the road to another L.V.G. which was returning to its lines, attacked it from above in front, tacked over it, reached its rear, and overwhelmed it like a thunder-clap. The Boche fell in flames between Assevillers and Herbécourt. One more victory, and this one had the honour of appearing in the official communiqué. Sometimes he got back with his machine and his clothes riddled with bullet-holes. He carried fire and massacre up into the sky. And all this was nothing as yet but the exercise of a knight-errant in his infancy. This became evident later when he had acquired complete mastery of his work.

February, 1916—the month in which began the longest, the most stubborn and cruel, and perhaps the most significant battle of the Great War. In this month began Verdun, and the menacing German advance on the right of the Meuse (February 21-26), to the wood of Haumont, the wood of the Caures and Herbebois, then to Samogneux, the wood of the Fosses, the Le Chaume wood and Ornes, and finally, on February 25, the attack on Louvemont and Douaumont. The escadrilles, little by little, headed in the same direction, and Guynemer was about to leave the Sixth Army. He would dart no more above the paternal mansion, announcing his victories by his caracoles in the air; nor watch over his own household during his patrol of the region beyond Compiègne, over Noyon, Chauny, Coucy, and Tracy-le-Val. The cord which still linked him with his infancy and youth was now to be strained, and on March 11 the Storks Escadrille received orders to depart next day, and to fly to the Verdun region.

The development of the German fighting aeroplanes had constantly progressed during 1915. Now, early in 1916, they appeared at Verdun, more homogeneous and better trained, and in possession of a series of new machines: small, one-seated biplanes (Albatros, Halberstadt, new Fokker, and Ago), with a fixed motor of 165-175 H.P. (Mercédès, and more rarely Benz and Argus), and two stationary machine-guns firing through the propeller. These chasing escadrilles (*Jagdstaffeln*) are essentially fighting units. Each *Jagdstaffeln* comprises eighteen aeroplanes, and sometimes twenty-two, four of which are reserves. These aeroplanes do not generally travel alone, at least when they have to leave their lines, but fly in groups (*Ketten*) of five each, one of them serving as guide (*Kettenfuhrer*), and conducted by the most experienced pilot, regardless of rank. German aviation tactics seek more and more to avoid solitary combat and replace it by squadron fighting, or to surprise an isolated enemy by a squadron, like an attack of sparrow-hawks upon an eagle.

Ever since the establishment of our first autonomous group of fighting aeroplanes, which figured in the Artois offensives in May, 1915, but which did not take the offensive (having their cantonments in the barriers and limiting themselves to keeping off the enemy and cruising above our lines and often behind them), our fighting aeroplanes gradually overcame prejudice. They were not, it is true, so promptly brought to perfection as our army corps aeroplanes, which proved so useful in the Champagne campaign of September, 1915; but it was admitted that the aerial combat should not be regarded as a result of mere chance, but as inevitable, and that it constituted, first, a protection, and afterwards an effective obstruction to an enemy forbidden to make raids in our aerial domain. The next German offensive—against Verdun—had been foreseen. In consequence, the staff had organized a safety service to avoid all surprise by the enemy, to meet attacks, and prepare the way for the reinforcing troops. But the violence of the Verdun offensive exceeded all expectations.

Our escadrilles had done their duty as scouts before the attack. After it began, they were overwhelmed and numerically unable to perform all the aerial missions required. The fighting enemy escadrilles, with their new series of machines and their improvements, won for a few days the complete mastery of the air. Our own aeroplanes were forced off the battlefield, and driven from their landing-places by cannon. Meanwhile the Verdun battle was changing its character. General Pétain, who took command on February 26, restored the order which had been compromised by the bending of the front, and established the new front against which the Germans hurled their forces. It was also necessary for him to reconquer the mastery of the air. He asked for and obtained a rapid concentration of all the available escadrilles, and demanded of them vigorous offensive tactics. To economize and coordinate strength, all the fighting escadrilles at Verdun were grouped under the sole command of Major de Rose. They operated by patrols, sometimes following very distant itineraries, and attacking all the aeroplanes they met. In a short time we regained our air supremacy, and our aeroplanes which were engaged in regulating artillery fire and in taking aerial photographs could work in safety. Their protection was assured by raids even into the German lines.

The Storks Escadrille, then, flew in the direction of Verdun. In the course of the voyage, Guynemer brought down his eighth aeroplane, which fell vertically in flames. This was a good augury. Hardly had he arrived on March 15 when he began to explore the battlefield with his conqueror's eyes. The enemy at that time still thought himself master, and dared to venture within the French lines. Guynemer chased, over Revigny, a group of five aeroplanes, drove another out of Argonne, and while returning met two others, almost face to face. He engaged the first one, tacking under it and firing from a distance of ten metres. But the adversary answered his fire, and Guynemer's machine was hit: the right-hand rear longitudinal spar was cut, the cable injured, the right forward strut also cut, and the wind-shield shattered. The airman himself was wounded in the face by fragments of aluminium and iron, one lodging in the jaw, from which it could never be extracted, one in the right cheek, one in the left eyelid, miraculously leaving the eye unhurt, while smaller fragments peppered him generally, causing haemorrhages which clogged his mask and made it adhere to the flesh. In addition, he had two bullets in his left arm. Though blinded by blood, he did not lose his sang-froid, and hastily dived, while the second aeroplane continued firing, and a third, furnished with a turret, which had come to the rescue of its comrades, descended after him and fired down upon his machine. Nevertheless, he had escaped by his manoeuvre, and in spite of his injuries made a good landing at Brocourt. On the 14th he was evacuated to Paris, to the Japanese ambulance in the Hotel Astoria, and with despair in his soul was obliged to let his comrades fight their battle of Verdun without his help.

CHAPTER 3

"La Terre a Vu Jadis Errer Des Paladins...."[19]

At Verdun our aerial as well as our land forces underwent sudden and almost prodigious reverses. Within a few days the Storks Escadrille had been decimated: its chief, Captain Brocard, had been wounded in the face by a bullet and compelled to land; Lieutenant Perretti had been killed, Lieutenant Deullin wounded, Guynemer wounded and nearly all its best pilots put hors de combat. The lost air-mastery was only regained by the tenacity of Major de Rose, Chief of Aviation of the Second Army, and by a rapid re-concentration of forces.

Major de Rose ordered enemy-chasing, and electrified and inspired his escadrilles. The part he played during those terrible Verdun months can never be sufficiently praised. Guynemer's comrades held the sky under fire, as their brothers, the infantrymen, held the shifting ground which protected the ancient citadel. Chaput brought down seven aeroplanes, Nungesser six, and a *drachen*, Navarre four, Lenoir four, Auger and Pelletier d'Oisy three, Puple, Chainat, and Lesort two. The observation aeroplanes rivalled the fighting machines, often defending themselves, and not infrequently forcing down their assailants in flames. Twice Sergeant Fedoroff rid himself in this manner of troublesome adversaries. But other pilots deserve to be mentioned, pilots such as Stribick and Houtt, Captain Vuillemin, Lieutenant de Laage, Sergeants de Ridder, Viallet and Buisse, and such observers as Lieutenant Liebmann, who was killed, and Mutel, Naudeau, Campion, Moulines, Dumas, Robbe, Travers, *sous-lieutenant* Boillot, Captain

---

19: "Once knightly heroes wandered over earth...."

Verdurand—admirable squadron chief—and Major Roisin, expert in bombardments. The lists of names are always too short, but these, at least, should be loudly acclaimed.

Meanwhile the battle of Verdun shattered trees, knocked down walls, annihilated villages, hollowed out the earth, dug up the plains, distorted the hills, and renewed once more that chaos of the third day, according to Genesis, on which the Creator separated the waters from the earth. Almost the entire French army filed through this extraordinary epic battle, and Guynemer, wounded and weeping with rage, was not there.

But there was another period in the Great War in which the grouping of our fighting escadrilles and their employment in offensive movements gave us triumphant superiority in the aerial struggle, and this was the battle of the Somme, particularly during its first three months—a splendid and heroic time when our airmen sprang up in the sky, spreading panic and fear, like the knights-errant of *La Légende des siècles*. Victor Hugo's verses seem to describe them and their vertiginous rounds rather than the too slow horsemen of old:

> *La terre a vu jadis errer des paladins;*
> *Ils flamboyaient ainsi que des éclairs soudains,*
> *Puis s'évanouissaient, laissant sur les visages*
> *La crainte, et la lueur de leurs brusques passages...*
> *Les noms de quelques-uns jusqu'à nous sont venus....*
> *Ils surgissaient du Sud ou du Septentrion,*
> *Portant sur leur écu l'hydre ou l'alérion,*
> *Couverts des noirs oiseaux du taillis héraldique,*
> *Marchant seuls au sentier que le devoir indique,*
> *Ajoutant au bruit sourd de leur pas solennel*
> *La vague obscurité d'un voyage éternel,*
> *Ayant franchi les flots, les monts, les bois horribles,*
> *Ils venaient de si loin qu'ils en étaient terribles,*
> *Et ces grands chevaliers mêlaient à leurs blazons*
> *Toute l'immensité des sombres horizons....*

These new knights-errant who wandered above the desolate plains of the Somme, no longer on earth but in the sky, mounted on winged steeds, who started up with a "heavy sound" from south or north, will be immortal like those of the ancient epics.

It will be said that it was Dormé or Heurtaux, or Nungesser, Deullin, Sauvage, Tarascon, Chainat, or it was Guynemer, who accomplished such and such an exploit. The Germans, without knowing their names, recognized them, not by their armour and their sword-thrust, but by their machines, their manoeuvres and methods. Almost invariably their enemies desperately avoided a fight with them, retreating far within their own lines, where, even then, they were not sure of safety. Those who accepted their gage of battle seldom returned. The enemy aviation camps from Ham to Péronne watched anxiously for the return of their champions who dared to fight over the French lines. None of them cared to fly alone, and even in groups they appeared timid. In patrols of four, five, and six, sometimes more, they flew beyond their own lines with the utmost caution, fearful at the least alarm, and anxiously examining the wide and empty sky where these mysterious knights mounted guard and might at any moment let loose a storm. But in the course of these prodigious first three months of the battle of the Somme, our French chasing-patrols not infrequently flew to and fro for two hours over German aviation camps, forcing down all those who attempted to rise, and succeeding in spreading terror and consternation in the enemy's lines.

The Franco-British offensive began on July 1, 1916, on the flat lands lying along both banks of the Somme River. The general plan of these operations had been agreed upon in the preceding December. The battle of Verdun had not prevented its execution which, on the contrary, was expected to relieve Verdun. The attack was made on a front of 40 kilometres between Gommécourt on the north and Vermandovillers on the south of the river. From the beginning the French penetrated the enemy's first lines, the 20th Corps took the village of Curlu and held the Favière wood, while the 1st Colonial Corps and one division of the 35th Corps passed the Fay ravine and took possession of Bacquincourt, Dompierre and Bussus. On the third, this successful advance continued into the second lines. Within just a few days General Fayolle's army had taken 10,000 prisoners, 75 cannon, and several hundred machine-guns. But the Germans, who were concentrated in the Péronne region, with strong positions like Maurepas, Combles, and Cléry, and, further in the rear, Bouchavesnes and Sailly-Sail-lisel on the right bank, and Estrées, Belloy-en-Santerre, Barleux, Albaincourt and Pressoire on the left bank, made such desperate resistance that the struggle was prolonged into mid-winter. The German retreat in March, 1917, to the famous Hindenburg line was the strategic result of this terrible battle, the tactics of which were continuously successful and the connection between the different arms brought to perfection, while the infantry made an unsurpassed record for suffering and endurance and will power in such combats as Maurepas (August 12), Cléry (September 3), Bouchavesnes (September 12)—where, when evening came, the enemy was definitely broken—and the taking of Berny-en-San-terre, of Deniécourt, of Vermandovillers (September 13) on the left bank, and on the right bank the entry into Combles (sur-rounded on September 26), the advance on Sailly-Saillisel and the stubborn defence of this ruined village whose château and central district had already been occupied on October 15, and in which a few houses resisted until November 12. Then, there was the fight for the Chaulnes wood, and La Maisonnette and Ablain-court and Pressoire; and everywhere it was the same as at Verdun: the woods were razed to the ground, villages disappeared into the soil, and the earth was so ploughed and crushed and martyred that it was nothing but one immense wound.

Now, the air forces had had their part in the victory. Obliged, as they were at Verdun, to resist the numerical superiority of the enemy, they had thrown off the tyranny of atmospheric condi-tions and accepted and fulfilled diverse missions in all kinds of weather. Verdun had hardened them, as it had "burned the blood" of the infantry who had never known a worse hell than that one. But as our operations now took the initiative, the aviation corps was able to prepare its material more effectively, to organize its aerodromes and concentrate its forces beforehand. Its advantage was evident from the first day of the Somme offensive, not only in mechanical power, but in a method which coordinated and increased its efforts under a single command. Though this arm of the service was in continuous evolution, more subject than any other to the modifications of the war, and the most susceptible of all to progress and improvement, it had nevertheless finished its trial stages and acquired full development as connecting agent for all the other arms, whom it supplied with information. Serving at first for strategic reconnaissance, and then almost exclusively for regulating artillery fire, the aerial forces now performed complex and efficient service for every branch of the army. By means of aerial photography they furnished exact knowledge of the ground and of the enemy's defences, thus preceding the execution of military operations. They regulated artillery fire, followed the program laid down for the destruction of the enemy, and supplied such information as was necessary to set the time for the attack. They then accompanied the infantry in the attack, observed its progress, located the conquered positions, revealed the situation of the enemy's new lines, betrayed his defensive works, and announced his reinforcements and his counter-attacks. They were the conducting wire between the command, the artillery, and the troops, and everybody felt them to be sure and faithful allies, for they were able to see and know, to speak and warn. But the air forces, during all their useful missions, were themselves in need of protection, and there must be no enemy aeroplanes about if they were to make their observations in security. But how to rid them of these enemies, and render the latter incapable of harm? Here the air cavalry, the aeroplanes built for distant scouting and combats, intervened. The safety of observation machines could only be insured by long-distance protection, that is to say, by aerial patrols taking the offensive, not by a solitary guard, too often disappointing, and ineffective against a resolute adversary. Their safety near to the army could be guaranteed only by carrying the aerial struggle over into the enemy's lines and preventing all raids upon our own. The groups belonging to our fighting escadrilles on both banks of the Somme achieved this result.

The one-seated Nieuport, rapid, easily managed, with high ascensional speed, and capable, by its solid construction and air-piercing power, of diving from a height upon an enemy and falling upon him like a bird of prey, was then the chasing aeroplane *par excellence*, and remained so until the appearance of the terrible Spad, which made its debut in the course of the Somme campaign, Guynemer and Corporal Sauvage piloting the first two of these machines in early September, 1916. They were armed with machine-guns, firing forward, and invariably connected with the direction of the machine's motion. The Spad is an extraordinary instrument of attack, but its defence lies only in its capacity for rapid displacement and the swiftness of its evolutions. Its rear is badly exposed: its field of visibility is very limited at the sides, and objects can be seen only above and below,—below, minus the dead angle of the motor and the cockpit. The pilot can easily lose sight of the aeroplanes in his own group or that of the enemy, so that if he is alone, he is in danger of being surprised. On the other hand, one condition of his own victory is to surprise the enemy, especially if he attacks a two-seated machine whose range of fire is much broader, or if he does not hesitate to choose his victim from among a group. The Spad pilot makes use of the sun, of fog, of clouds. He flies high in order to hold the advantage of being able to pounce down upon his enemy while the enemy approaches prudently, timidly, suspecting no danger.

The battle of the Somme was the most favourable for solitary aeroplanes, or aeroplanes coupled like hunting-dogs. Since then methods have changed, and the future belongs to fighting escadrilles or groups of machines. But at that time the one-seated aeroplane was king of the air. One of them was enough to intimidate enemy aeroplanes engaged in regulating artillery fire and in short-distance scouting, making them hesitate to leave their lines, and to frighten barrier patrols of two or even four two-seated aeroplanes, in spite of their shooting superiority, into turning back and disbanding. The one-seated enemy machines never ventured out except in groups, and even with the advantage of two against one refused to fight. So the one-seated French machine was obliged to fly alone, for if it was accompanied by patrols, the enemy fled and there was no one to attack; whereas, when free to manoeuvre at will, the solitary pilot could plan ruses, hide himself in the light or in the clouds, take advantage of the enemy's blind sides, and carry out sudden destructive attacks which are impossible for groups. Our airmen never speak of the Somme without a smile of satisfaction: they have retained heroic memories of that campaign. Afterwards, the Germans drilled their one-seated or two-seated patrols, trained them in resistance to isolated attacks, and taught them in turn how to attack the solitary machine which had ventured out beyond its own lines. We were obliged to alter our tactics and adopt group formation. But the strongest types of our enemy-chasing pilots were revealed or developed during the battle of the Somme.

Moreover, our aviators at that time were incomparable; and in citing the most illustrious among them one risks injustice to their companions whose opportunities were less fortunate and whose exploits were less brilliant but not less useful. The cavalry, artillery, and infantry were drawn upon for recruits for the aviation branch of the army, and it appeared a difficult undertaking to fuse such different elements; but as all shared the same life and the same dangers, had similar tastes, and a passion for attaining the same result, and as their officers were necessarily recruited from among themselves, and chosen for services rendered, an atmosphere of camaraderie and friendly rivalry was created. A great novelist said that the origin of our friendships dates—

> ... from those hours at the beginning of life when we dream
> of the future in company with some comrade with the same
> ideals as our own, a chosen brother.[20]

What difference does it make, then, if they depart in company for glory or for death? These young men gave themselves with the same willingness to the same service, a service full of constant danger. They were not gathered together by chance, but by their vocation and by selection, and they spoke the same language. For them, friendship easily became rivalry in courage and energy, and a school of mutual esteem, in which each strove to outdo the other. Friendship kept them alert, drove away inertia and weakness, and they became confident and generous, so that each rejoiced in the success of the others. In the mountains, on the sea, in every place where men feel most acutely their own fragility, such friendship is not rare; but war brings it to perfection.

The patrols of the Storks Escadrille, in the beginning of the Somme campaign, consisted of a single aeroplane, or aeroplanes in couples. Guynemer, whom everybody called "the kid," always took Heurtaux with him when he carried a passenger; for Heurtaux, as blond as Guynemer was brown, thin and slender, very delicate and young, seemed to give Guynemer the rights of an elder. Heurtaux was the Oliver of this Roland. In character and energy they were

---

20: Paul Bourget, *Une Idylle tragique.*

the same. Dormé used to take Deullin with him, or de la Tour. Or the choice was made alternately. This was the quartet of whom the enemy had cause to beware, and woe to the Boche who met any one of them! There was at that time at Bapaume a group of five one-seated German machines which never manoeuvred singly. If they perceived a pair of Nieuports, they immediately tacked about and fled in haste. But if one of our chasers was cruising alone, the whole group attacked him. Heurtaux, attacked in this way, had been compelled to dive and land, and on his return had to submit to the jests of Guynemer, for at that age friendship is roughish. "Go there yourself," advised Heurtaux, "and you will see."

Next day Guynemer went alone, but in his turn was forced down. After these two trials, which might have ended in disaster—but knights must amuse themselves—the five one-seated planes at Bapaume were methodically but promptly beaten down.

Friendship demands equality between souls. If one has to protect the other, if one is manifestly superior, it is no longer friendship. In the Storks Escadrille friendship reigned in peace in the midst of war, so surely did each take his turn in surpassing the others. Which one was, finally, to be the greatest, not because of the number of his mentions, nor his renown or public fame, but according to the testimony of his comrades—the surest and most clear-sighted of testimony—for no one can deceive his peers? Would it be the cold and calm Dormé, who went to battle as a fisher goes to his nets, who never spoke of his exploits, and whose heart, under this modest, gentle, kind exterior, was filled with hatred for the invader who occupied his own countryside, Briey, and for six months had held in custody and ill-treated his parents? In the Somme battle alone his official victories numbered seventeen, but the enemy could recount many others, doubtless, for this silent, well-balanced young man possessed quite improbable audacity. He would fly more than fifteen or twenty kilometres above the German lines, perfectly tranquil under the showers of shells which rose from the earth. At such a distance within their lines the Boche aeroplanes thought themselves safe when, suddenly, *du Sud ou du Septentrion*, appeared this knightly hero. And he would return smilingly, as fresh as when he had started out. It was only with difficulty that a very brief statement could then be extracted

IN THE AIR

from him. His machine would be inspected, and not a trace of any fragment found; he might have been a tourist returning from a promenade. In more than a hundred combats his aeroplane received only three very small wounds. His cleverness in handling his machine was incredible: his close veering, his twistings and turnings, made it impossible for the adversary to shoot. He also knew how to quit the combat in time, if his own manoeuvres had not succeeded. He seemed invulnerable. But later, much later, while he was fighting on the Aisne in May, 1917, Dormé, who had penetrated far within the enemy's lines, never came back.

Was Heurtaux the greatest, whose method was as delicate as himself—a virtuoso of the air, clever, supple and quick-witted, whose hand and eye equalled his thought in rapidity? Was it Deullin, skilled in approach, and prompt as the tempest? Or the long-enduring, robust, admirable *sous-lieutenant* Nungessor, or Sergeant Sauvage, or Adjutant Tarascon? Was it Captain Ménard, or Sangloer, or de la Tour? But the reader knows very well that it was Guynemer. Why was it Guynemer, according to the testimony of all his rivals? History and the epic have coupled many names of friends, like Achilles and Patroclus, Orestes and Pylades, Nisus and Euryalus, Roland and Oliver. In these friendships, one is always surpassed by the other, but not in intelligence, nor courage nor nobility of character. For generosity, or wisdom of council, one might even prefer a Patroclus to an Achilles, an Oliver to a Roland. In what, then, lies the superiority? That is the secret of temperament, the secret of genius, the interior flame which burns the brightest, and whose appearances cause astonishment and almost terror, as if some mystery were divulged.

It is certain that Georges Guynemer was a mechanician and a gunsmith. He knew his machine and his machine-gun, and how to make them do their utmost. But there were others who knew the same. Dormé and Heurtaux were perhaps more skilful in manoeuvring than he. (It was interesting to watch Guynemer when he was preparing to mount his Nieuport. First the bird was brought out of the shed; then he minutely examined and fingered it. This tall thin young man, with his amber-coloured skin, his long oval face and thin nose, his mouth with its corners falling slightly, a very slight moustache, and crow-black hair tossed backward, would have resembled a Moorish chief had he been more impassive. But his features constantly showed his changing thoughts, and this play of expression gave grace and freshness to his face. Sometimes it seemed strained and hardened, and a vertical wrinkle appeared on his forehead above the nose. His eyes— the unforgettable eyes of Guynemer—round like agates, black and burning with a brilliance impossible to endure, for which there is only one expression sufficiently strong, that of Saint-Simon concerning some personage of the court of Louis XIV: "The glances of his eyes were like blows"—pierced the sky like arrows, when his practiced ear had heard the harsh hum of an enemy motor. In advance he condemned the audacious adversary to death, seeming from a distance to draw him into the abyss, like a sorcerer.) After examining his machine he put on his fur-lined *combinaison* over his black coat, and his head-covering, the *passe-montagne*, fitting tightly over his hair, and framing the oval of his face, and over this his leather helmet. Plutarch spoke of the terrible expression of Alexander when he went to battle. Guynemer's face, when he rose for a flight, was appalling.

What did he do in the air? His flight journals and statements tell the story. On each page, a hundred times in succession, and several times on a page, his flight notebooks contain the short sentences which seem to bound from the paper, like a dog showing its teeth: "I attack ... I attack ... I attack...." At long intervals, as if ashamed, appears the phrase: "I am attacked."

On the Somme more than twenty victories were credited to him, and to these should be added, as in the case of Dormé, others taking place at too great distances to receive confirmation. In the first month of the Somme battle, on September 13, 1916, the Storks Escadrille, Captain Brocard, was mentioned before the army:

> Has shown unequalled energy and devotion to duty in the operations of Verdun and the Somme, waging, from March 19 to August 19, 1916, 338 combats, bringing down 36 aeroplanes, 3 *drachen*, and compelling 36 other badly damaged aeroplanes to land.

Captain Brocard dedicated this mention to Lieutenant Guynemer, writing under it:

To Lieutenant Guynemer, my oldest pilot, and most brilliant Stork. Souvenir of gratitude and warmest friendship.

And all the pilots of the escadrille, in turn, came to sign it. His comrades had often seen what he did in the air.

When Guynemer came back and landed, what a spectacle! Although a victor, his face was not appeased. It was never to be appeased. He never was satisfied, never waged enough battles, never burned or destroyed enough enemies. When he landed he was still under the influence of nervous effort, and seemed as if electrified by the fluid still passing through his frame. However, his machine bore traces of the struggle: four bullets in the wing, the body, and the elevator. And he himself was grazed by the missiles, his *combinaison* scratched and the end of his glove torn. By what miracle had he escaped?—He had passed through encircling death as a man leaps through a hoop.

His method was one of the wildest temerity and impetuosity, and can be recommended to nobody. The number and strength of the enemy, so far from repelling, attracted him. He flew to vertiginous heights, and taking his place in the sunshine, watched and waited. In an attack he did not make use of the aerial acrobatic manoeuvres with which, however, he was perfectly familiar. He struck without delay,—what is known in fencing as the cut direct. Without trying to maintain his machine within his adversary's dead angles, he fell on him as a stone falls. He shot as near to the enemy as he could, at the risk of being shot first himself, and even of interlocking their machines, though in that respect the sureness of his manoeuvring sufficed to disengage him. If he failed to take the enemy by surprise, he did not quit the combat as prudence exacted; but returned to the charge, refusing to unhook his clutch from the enemy aeroplane, and held him, and wanted him, and got him.

His passion for flying never diminished. On rainy days, when it was unreasonable and useless to attempt to fly, he wandered around the sheds where the winged horses took their repose. He could not resist it: he entered, and mounted his own machine, settling himself in his cock-pit and handling the controls, holding mysterious con-

21: Flaubert.

93

ferences with his faithful steed.

In the air, he had a higher power of resistance than the most robust men. This frail, sickly Guynemer, twice refused by the army because of feebleness of constitution, never gave up. In proportion as the requirements of aviation became more severe, as the higher altitudes reached made it more exhausting, Guynemer seemed to prolong his flights to the point where overwork and nervous depression compelled him to go away and take a little rest—which made him suffer still more. And suddenly, before he had taken the necessary repose, he threw it off like ballast, and returning to camp, reappeared in the air, like the falcon in the legend of Saint Julien the Hospitaller:

> The bold bird rose straight in the air like an arrow, and there could be seen two spots of unequal size which turned and joined, and then disappeared in the heights of heaven. The falcon soon descended, tearing some bird to pieces, and returned to his perch on the gauntlet, with his wings quivering.[21]

Thus the victorious Guynemer came back, quivering, to the aviation field. Truly, a god possessed him. Apart from all that, he was just a boy, simple, gay, tender, and charming.

CHAPTER 4

On the Somme
June, 1916, to February, 1917

Georges Guynemer, then, was wounded on March 15, 1916, at Verdun. On April 26, he arrived again at the front, with his arm half-cured and the wounds scarcely healed. He had escaped from the doctors and nurses. Between times, he had been promoted *sous-lieutenant*. But he had to be sent back, to his bandages and massage.

He returned to Compiègne. The bargain he had made with his sister Yvonne was continued, and when the weather was clear he went to Vauciennes, where his machine awaited him. The first time he met an aeroplane after his fall and his wound, he experienced a quite natural but very painful sensation. Would he hesitate? Was he no longer the stubborn Guynemer? The Boche shot, but he did not reply. The Boche used up all his machine-gun belt, and the combat was broken off. Was it to be believed? What had happened?

Guynemer returned to his home. In the spring dawn comes very soon, and he had left so early that it was still morning. Was his sister awake? He waited, but waiting was not his forte. So he opened the door again, and his childish face appeared in the strip of light that filtered through. This time the sleeper saw him.

"Already back? Go back to bed. It is too early."

"Is it really so early?"

Her sisterly tenderness divined that he had something to tell her, something important, and that it would be necessary to help him to tell it. "Come in," she said.

He opened the blinds and sat down at the foot of the bed.

"What scouting have you done this morning?"

But he was following his own thoughts: "The men had warned me that under those circumstances one receives a very disagreeable impression."

"Under what circumstances?"

"When one goes up again after having been wounded, and meets a Boche. As long as you have not been wounded you think nothing can happen to you. When I saw that Boche this morning I felt something quite new. Then...."

He stopped and laughed, as if he had played some schoolboy joke.

"Then, what did you do?"

"Well, I made up my mind to submit to his shots. Calmly."

"Without replying?"

"Surely: I ordered myself not to shoot. That is the way one masters one's nerves, little sister. Mine are entirely mastered: I am now absolutely in control. The Boche presented me with five hundred shots while I manoeuvred. They were necessary. I am perfectly satisfied."

She looked at him, sitting at the foot of the bed with his head resting against the post. Her eyes were wet and she kept silent. The silence continued.

Finally she said softly, "You have done well, Georges."

But he was asleep.

Later, referring to this meeting in which he offered himself to the enemy's fire, he said gravely:

"That was the decisive moment of my life. If I had not set things right then and there, I was done for...."

When he reappeared at his escadrille's head-quarters on May 18, quite cheerful but with a set face and flaming eyes, no one dared discuss his cure with him.

The Storks returned for a few days to the Oise region, and once more the contented pilot of a Nieuport flew over the country from Péronne to Roye. He had not lost the least particle of his determination; quite the reverse. One day (May 22) he searched the air desperately for three hours, and though he finally discovered a two-seated enemy machine over Noyon, he was obliged to give over the combat for lack of gasoline in his motor.

Meanwhile they were preparing the Somme battle; the escadrilles familiarized themselves with their ground, and new machines were tried. The enemy, who suspected our preparations, sent out long-distance scouting aeroplanes. Near Amiens, above Villers-Bretonneux, Guynemer, making his rounds with Sergeant Chainat, attacked one of these groups on June 22, isolated one of the aeroplanes and, manoeuvring with his comrade, set it afire. That was, I believe, his ninth. This combat took place at a height of 4200 metres. The advantage went more and more to the pilot who mounted highest.

After July 1 there was a combat almost every day. Would Guynemer be put out of action from the beginning, as at Verdun? Returning on the 6th, after having put to flight an L.V.G., he surprised another Boche aeroplane which was diving down on one of our artillery-regulating machines. He immediately drew the enemy's attention to himself; but the enemy (Guynemer pays him this homage in his flight notebook) was keen and supple. His well-aimed shots passed through the propeller of the Nieuport and cut two cables in the right cell. Guynemer was obliged to land. He was forced down eight times during his flying career, once under fantastic conditions. He passed through every form of danger without ever losing the self-possession, the quickness of eye, and rapidity of decision which his passion for conquest had developed.

What battles he fought in the air! On July 9 his journal notes a combat of five against five; on the 10th a combat of three against seven, in which Guynemer disengaged Deullin, who was followed by an Aviatik at a distance of a hundred metres. On the 11th, at 10 o'clock, he attacked an L.V.G. and cut its cable; the enemy dived but appeared to be in control of the machine. A few moments later he and Deullin attacked an Aviatik and an L.V.G., Guynemer damaging the Aviatik, and Deullin forcing down the L.V.G.; and before returning to their base, the two comrades attacked a group of seven machines and dispersed them. On the 16th Guynemer forced down, with Heurtaux, an L.V.G., which fell with its wheels in the air. After a short absence, during which he got a more powerful machine for his own use, he began on the 25th a repetition of his former program. On the 26th he waged five combats with enemy groups consisting of from five to eleven aeroplanes. On the 27th he fought three L.V.G.'s, and then groups of from three to ten machines. On the 28th he successively attacked two aeroplanes within their own lines, then a *drachen* which was obliged to land, then a group of four aeroplanes one of which was forced down, and then a second group of four which were dispersed, Guynemer pursuing one of the fugitives and bringing him down. One blade of his own propeller was riddled with bullets, and he was compelled to land. Such was his work for three days, taken at random from the notebook.

Open his journal at any page, and it reads the same. On August 7 Guynemer got back with seven shell fragments in his machine: he had been cannonaded from the ground while in chase of four enemy aeroplanes. On the same day he started off again, piloting Heurtaux, who attacked the German trenches north of Cléry and fired on some machine-guns. From its place up in the air the aeroplane encouraged the infantry, and shared in their assaults. The recital of events became, however, more and more brief: the fighting pilot had not time enough to write details; nobody had any time in the Storks Escadrille, constantly engaged as it was in its triumphant flights. We must turn then to Guynemer's letters—strange letters, indeed, which contain nothing, absolutely nothing about the war, or the battle of the Somme, or about anything else except *his* war and *his* battle. The earth-world no longer existed for him: the earth was a place which received the dead and the vanquished. So this is the way in which he wrote his two sisters, then sojourning in Switzerland (Fritz meaning any enemy aeroplane):

Dear Kids,

Some sport: the 17, attacked a Fritz, three shots and gun jammed; Fritz tumbled. The 18th, *idem*, but in two shots: two Fritzes in five shots, record.

Day before yesterday, attacked Fritz at 4.30 at ten metres: killed the passenger and perhaps the rest, prevented from seeing what happened by a fight at half-past four: the Boche ran.

At 7.40 attacked an Aviatik, carried away by the impetus, passed it at fifty centimetres; passenger *couic* (killed), the machine fell and was got under control again at fifty metres above the ground.

At 7.35, attacked an L.V.G.; at fifteen metres; just ready to shoot, when a bullet in my fingers made me let go the trigger; reservoir burst, good landing two kilometres from the trenches between two shell-holes. Inventory of the "taxi": one bullet right in the face of my Vickers; one perforative bullet in the motor; the steel stone had gone clear through it as well as the oil reservoir, the gasoline tank, the cartridge chest, my glove … where it stayed in the index finger: result, about as if my finger had been slightly pinched in a door; not even skinned, only the top of the nail slightly blackened. At the time I thought two fingers had been shot. To continue the inventory: one bullet in the reservoir, in the direction of my left lung, having passed through four millimetres of copper and had the good sense to stop, but one wonders why.

One bullet in the edge of the back of my seat, one in the rudder, and a dozen in the wings. They knocked the "taxi" to pieces with a hatchet at two o'clock in the morning, under shell-fire. On landing, received 86 shots of 105, 130 and 150, for nothing. They will pay the bill.

For a beginning, La Tour has his fourth mention.

A hug for each of you.

Georges

P.S.—It could not be said now that I am not strong; I stop steel bullets with the end of my finger.

Is this a letter? At first, it is a bulletin of victory: two aeroplanes for five bullets, plus one passenger *couic*. Then it becomes a recital of the golden legend—the golden legend of aviation: he stops the enemy's bullets with his fingers; Roland would write in that style to the beautiful Aude:

Met three Saracens, Durandal cleft two, the third tried to settle the affair with his bow, but the arrow broke on the cord.

Young Paul Bailly was right:

The exploits of Guynemer are not a legend, like those of Roland; in telling them just as they happened we find them more beautiful than any we could invent.

That is why it is better to let Guynemer himself relate them. He says only what is necessary, but the right accent is there, the rapidity and the *couic*. The following letter, also to his sisters, is dated September 15, 1916.

Some sport.

On the 16th, in a group of six, four of them squeezed at 25 metres.

In four days, six combats at 25 metres: filled a few Boches with holes, but they did not seem to tumble down, though some were hard hit all the same; then five boxing rounds up between 5100 and 5300 (altitude). Today five combats, four of them at less than 25 metres, and the fifth at 50 metres. In the first, gun jammed at 50 metres. In the second, at 5200, the Boche in his excitement lost his wings, and descended on his aerodrome in a wingless coach; his ears must be humming (16th). The third was a nose-to-nose combat with a fighting Aviatik. Too much impetus: I failed to hammer him hollow. In the fourth, same joke with an L.V.G. in a group of three: I failed to hammer him, I lurched: *pan*, a bullet near my head. In the fifth, I cleaned up the passenger (that is the third this week), then knocked up the pilot very badly at 10 metres,—completely disabled, he landed evidently with great difficulty, and he must be in hospital....

Three lines to describe a victory, the sixteenth. And what boarding of the adversary, from above and from below! He springs upon the enemy, but fails to go through him. Both speeds combined, he does not make much less than 400 kilometres an hour when he dives on him. The meeting and shooting hardly last one second, after which the combat continues, with other manoeuvres. Some savant should calculate the time allowed for sight and thought in fighting such duels!

This was the period of the great series of combats on the Somme. The Storks Escadrille, which was the first to arrive, waged battle uninterruptedly for eight months. Other escadrilles came to the rescue. Altogether they were divided into two groups, one under the command of Major Féquant, the other under that of Captain Brocard, appointed chief of battalion. It becomes impossible to enumerate all Guynemer's victories, and we can merely emphasize the days on which he surpassed himself. September 28 was a remarkable day, on which he brought down two enemies and had a fall from a height of 3000 metres. Little Paul Bailly would hardly have believed that; he would have said it was surely a legend, the golden legend of aviation. Nevertheless, here is Guynemer's statement, countersigned by the escadrille commandant:

> *Saturday, September 23.*—Two combats near Eterpigny. At 11.20 forced down a Boche in flames near Aches; at 11.21 forced a Boche to land, damaged, near Carrépuy; at 11.25 forced down a Boche in flames near Roye. At 11.30, was forced down myself by a French shell, and smashed my machine near Fescamps....

These combats occurred between Péronne and Montdidier. To his father he wrote with more precision, but in his usual elliptical style.

> *September 22*: Asphyxiated a Fokker in 30 seconds, tumbled down disabled.

> *September 23*: 11.20.—A Boche in flames within our lines.

> 11.21.—A Boche disabled, passenger killed.

> 11.25.—A Boche in flames 400 metres from the lines.

> 11.25 and a half.—A 75 blew up my water reservoir, and all the linen of the left upper plane, hence a superb tail spin. Succeeded in changing it into a glide. Fell to ground at speed of 160 or 180 kilometres: everything broken like matches, then the 'taxi' rebounded, turned around at 45 degrees, and came back, head down, planting itself in the ground 40 metres away like a post; they could not budge it. Nothing was left but the body, which was intact: the Spad is strong; with any other machine I should now be thinner than this sheet of paper. I fell 100 metres from the battery that had demolished me; they had not aimed at me, but they brought me down all the same, which they had no difficulty in recognizing; the shell struck me hard some time before exploding. The Boche fell close by Major Constantin's post. I picked up the pieces.

The group which he had attacked was composed of five aeroplanes, flying in *échelon*, three above, two below. The two which flew lowest were assaulted by one of our escadrilles, and the pilots, seeing a machine fall in flames, thought at first it was their own victory.

"It was my first one, falling from the upper story," Guynemer explained drolly, in his Stanislas-student manner. With his "*terrible oiseau*" he had waged battle with the three pilots "of the upper story," and had forced them down one after the other. "The first one," he said, "had a half-burned card in his pocket which had certainly been given him that same morning, judging by the date, which read in German: 'I think you are very successful in aviation.' I have his photograph with his Gretchen. What German heads! He wore the same decorations as that one who fell in the Bus wood...."

Is this not Achilles setting his foot on Hector and taking possession of his trophies? Guynemer's heart was stone to his enemies. He saw in them the wrongs done to France, the invasion of our country, the destruction of our towns and villages, our desolation, and our dead, so many of our dead whose deserted homes weep for them. His was not to give pity, but to do justice. And in doing justice, when an adversary whom he had forced down was wounded, he brought him help with all his native generosity.

For him, thirty seconds had separated the Capitol from the Tarpeian Rock. After his triple victory came his incredible fall, unheard of, fantastic, from a height of 3000 metres, the Spad falling at the highest speed down to earth, and rebounding and planting itself in the ground like a picket.

I was completely stupefied for twenty-four hours, but have escaped with merely immense fatigue (especially where I wear my looping-the-loop straps, which saved my life), and a gash in my knee presented to me by my magneto. During that 3000-meter tumble I was planning the best way to hit the ground (I had the choice of sauces): I found the way, but there were still 95 out of 100 chances for the wooden cross. *Enfin*, all right!

And this postscript followed:

Sixth time I have been brought down: record!

Lieutenant V.F., of the Dragon Escadrille, colliding with a comrade's aeroplane at a height of 3000 metres, had a similar fall onto the Avocourt wood, and was similarly astounded to find himself whole. He had continued manoeuvring during the five or six minutes of the descent. He wrote:

Soon the trees of the Hesse forest came in sight; in fact, they seemed to approach at a dizzy rate of speed. I switched off so as not to catch fire, and a few metres before reaching the trees I nosed up my machine with all my strength so that it would fall flat. There was a terrible shock! One tree higher than the rest broke my right wings, and made me turn as if I were on a pivot. I closed my eyes. There was a second shock, less violent than I could have hoped: the machine fell on its nose like a stone, at the foot of the tree which had stopped me. I unfastened my belt which, luckily, had not broken, and let myself slip onto the ground, amazed not to be suffering intense agony. The only bad effects were that my head was heavy, and blood was flowing through my mask. I breathed, coughed, and shook my arms and legs, and was dumbfounded to find that all my faculties functioned normally....

Guynemer did not tell us so much; but, as a mathematician, he calculated his chances. He too had switched off, and with the greatest sang-froid superintended, so to speak, his fall. Its result was no less magical.

The infantrymen had observed this rainfall of aeroplanes. The French plane reached the earth just before its pilot's last victim fell also, in flames. The soldiers pitied the poor victor, who had not, as they thought, survived his conquest! They rushed to his aid, expecting to pick him up crushed to atoms. But Guynemer stood up without aid. He seemed like a ghost; but he was standing, he was alive, and the excited soldiers took possession of him and carried him off in triumph. A division general approached, and immediately commanded a military salute for the victor, saying to Guynemer:

"You will review the troops with me."

Guynemer did not know how to review troops, and would have liked to go. He was suffering cruelly from his knee:

"I happen to be wounded, General."

"Wounded, you! It's impossible. When a man falls from the sky without being broken, he is a magician, no doubt of that. You cannot be wounded. However, lean upon me."

And holding him up, almost indeed carrying him, he walked with the young *sous-lieutenant* in front of the troops. From the neighbouring trenches rose the sound of singing, first half-suppressed, and then swelling into a formidable roar: the *Marseillaise.* The song had sprung spontaneously to the men's lips.

* * * * * * * *

Cerebral commotion required Guynemer to rest for a few days. But on October 5 he started off again. The month of October on the Somme was marked by an improvement in German aviation, their numbers being considerably reinforced and supplied with new tactics. Guynemer defied the new tactics of numbers, and in one day, October 17, attacked a group of three one-seated planes, and another group of five. A second time he made a sortie, and attacked a two-seated plane which was aided by five one-seated machines. On another occasion, November 9, he waged six battles with one-seated and two-seated machines, all of which made their escape, one after another, by diving. Still this was not enough, and he set forth again and attacked a group of one Albatros and four one-seated planes. "Hard fight," says the journal, "the enemy has the advantage."

He broke off this combat, but only to engage in another with an Albatros which had surprised Lieutenant Deullin at 50 metres. On the following day, November 10, he added two more items to his list (making his nineteenth and twentieth): his first victim, at whom he had shot fifteen times from a distance less than ten metres, fell in flames south of Nesle; the other, a two-seated Albatros, 220 H.P. Mercédès, protected by three one-seated machines, fell and was crushed to pieces in the Morcourt ravine. This double stroke he repeated on the twenty-second of the same month (making his twenty-second and twenty-third), and again on January 23, 1917 (his twenty-sixth and twenty-seventh), and still again the next day, the twenty-fourth (his twenty-eighth and twenty-ninth victories). In addition, here is one of his letters with a statement of the results of three chasing days. There are no longer headings or endings to his letters; he makes a direct attack, as he does in the air.

26-1-'17

January 24, 1917.—Fell on a group of five Boches at 2300. I brought them back, with drums beating, at 800 metres (one wire stay cut, one escape pot broken). At the end of the boxing-round, 400 metres above Roye, I succeeded in getting behind a one-seated machine of the group. My motor stopped; obliged to pump and let the Boche go.

11.45.—Attacked a Fritz, let him go at 800 metres, my motor spattered, but the Boche landed, head down, near Goyancourt. I only count him as damaged.

At this instant, I see a Boche cannonaded at 2400, hence at 11.50 a boxing round necessary with a little Rumpler armed with two machine-guns. The pilot got a bullet in his lung; the passenger, who fired at me, got one in his knee. The two reservoirs were hit, and the whole machine took fire and tumbled down at Lignières, within our lines. I landed alongside; in starting in again one wheel was broken in the ploughed frozen earth. In taking away the "taxi" the park people completely demolished it for me. It was rushed to Paris for repairs.

25.—I watch the others fly, and fume.

26.—Bucquet loaned me his "taxi." No viewfinder; only a wretchedly bad (oh, how bad!) sight-line.

At 12 o'clock.—Saw a Boche at 3800; took the lift.—Arrived at the sun.—In turning, was caught in an eddy-wind, rotten tail spin.—While coming down again I saw the Boche aiming at me 200 metres away; sent him ten shots: gun jammed; but the Boche seemed excited and dived with his motor in full blast straight south. Off we go! But I took care not to get too near so that he would not see that my gun was out of action. The altimeter tumbled: 1600 Estrées-Saint-Denis came in sight. I manoeuvred my Boche as well as I could. Suddenly he righted himself and departed in the direction of Rheims, banging away at me.

I tried bluffing; I rose 500 metres and let myself fall on him like a pebble. When I began to think my bluff had not succeeded, he seemed impressed and began to descend again. I placed myself at a distance of 10 metres, but every time I showed my nose the passenger aimed at me. The road to Compiègne: 1000 ... 800 metres. When I showed my nose, the passenger, standing, stopped aiming and made a sign that he gave himself up. All right! I saw under his belly that four shells had struck the mark. 400 metres: the Boche slowed up his "moulin" (motor). 200 metres, 20 metres. I let him go and watched him land. At 100 metres I circled and found I was over an aerodrome. But, having no more cartridges, I could not prevent them from setting fire to their "taxi," a magnificent 200 H.P. Albatros. When I saw they had been surrounded, I landed and showed the Boches my broken machine-gun. Sensation. They had fired at me two hundred times: my bullets, before the breakdown, had gone through their altimeter and their tachometer, which had caused their excitement. The pilot said that an aeroplane had been forced down two days before at Goyancourt: passenger killed, pilot wounded in legs—had to have one amputated above the knee. I hope this original confirmation will be accepted, which will make 30.

Thirty victories, twenty or twenty-one of which occurred on the Somme: such is the schedule of these extraordinary flights. The last one surpassed all the rest. He fought unarmed, with nothing but his machine, like a knight who, with sword broken, manages his horse and brings his adversary to bay. What a scene it was when the German pilot and passenger, prisoners, became aware that Guynemer's machine-gun had been out of action! Once more he had imposed his will upon others, and his power of domination had fascinated his enemies.

In the beginning of February, 1917, the Storks Escadrille left the Somme after six months' fighting, and flew into Lorraine.

GUYNEMER AND THE VIEUX CHARLES

BREUIL LE SEC

GUYNEMER IN 1917

GUYNEMER WITH HIS AIRCRAFT

GUYNEMER READY FOR ACTION

GUYNEMER AND THE VIEUX CHARLES

GUYNEMER AND THE VIEUX CHARLES

GUYNEMER AND GUERDER

GUYNEMER AND THE VIEUX CHARLES

OPPOSITE: GUYNEMER WITH HIS AIRCRAFT

GUYNEMER RECEIVING THE AWARD OF CHEVALIER OF THE LEGION OF HONOUR

At the Zenith

CHAPTER 1

On the 25th of May, 1917

The destiny of a Guynemer is to surpass himself. Part of his power, however, must lie in the perfection of his weapons. Why could he not forge them himself? In him, the mechanician and the gunsmith were impatient to serve the pilot and the fighter. Nothing in the science of aviation was unknown to him, and Guynemer in the factory was always the same Guynemer. He worked with the same nervous tension when he overhauled his machine-guns to avoid the too frequent and too troublesome jamming, or when he improved the arrangement of the instruments and tools in his aeroplane in accordance with his superior practical experience, as when he chased an enemy. He wanted to compel the obedience of matter, as he compelled the enemy to surrender.

In the Somme campaign he had forced down two aeroplanes in a single day, and then four in two days. In Lorraine he was to do even better. At that time, the beginning of 1917, the German aerial forces were very active in Lorraine, but the city of Nancy paid no attention to them. In 1914 Nancy had seen the invading army broken against the mountain of Saint Geneviève and the Grand Couronné; she had withstood a bombardment by gigantic shells and visits from air squadrons, and all without losing her good humour and her animation. She was one of those cities on the front who are accustomed to danger, and who find in it an inspiration for courage, for commerce, and even for pleasure which does not belong to cities behind the lines. Sometimes people who were dining on the Place Stanislas left their tables to watch some fine battle in the air, after which they resumed their seats and their appetites, merely replacing Rhenish by Moselle wines. Nevertheless, the frequency of raids, and the destruction caused by bombs, began to make the existence of both native and visiting Nancyites decidedly unpleasant. The Storks Escadrille, which arrived in February, very promptly punished these aerial brigands, by a police policy both rapid and severe. The enemy aeroplanes which flew over Nancy were vigorously chased, and less than a month later the framework of a good dozen of them, arranged in an orderly manner around the statue of Stanislas Leczinski, reassured the population and served as an interesting spectacle for the visitor who could no longer have the pleasure of admiring, behind Lamour's gates, the two monumental fountains consecrated to Neptune and Amphitrite, by Guibal, and which were then covered by coarse sacks of earth.

Guynemer had contributed his share of these *spolia opima*. On March 16 he alone had forced down three Boches, and a fourth on the 17th. Three victories in one day constituted a novel exploit. Navarre had achieved a double victory on February 26, 1916, at Verdun, and Guynemer had the same success on the Somme; in this campaign Nungesser had burned a *drachen* and two aeroplanes in one morning; but three aeroplanes destroyed in one day had never been seen before.

On that same evening Guynemer wrote to his family, and I transcribe the letter just as it is, with neither heading nor final formula. The King of Spain, in Ruy Blas, talks of the weather before he tells of the six wolves he has killed; but the new Cid fought in all weathers and speaks of nothing but his chase:

> *9 o'clock.*—Rose from the ground on hearing shell explosions. Forced down in flames a two-seated Albatros at 9.08.
>
> *9.20.*—Attacked with Deuillin a group of three one-seated Albatros, famous on the Lorraine front. At 9.26 I brought one down almost intact: pilot wounded, Lieutenant von Hausen, nephew of the general. And Deullin brought down another in flames at the same time. About 9 o'clock Dormé and Auger had attacked and grilled a two-seated plane. These four Boches were in a quadrilateral, the sides of which measured five kilometres, four and a half kilometres, three kilometres and three kilometres. Those who were in the middle need not have bothered themselves, but they were completely distracted.

14.30.—Forced down a two-seated Albatros in flames. Three Boches within our lines for my day's work.... *Ouf!* G. G.

Guynemer, who had been promoted lieutenant in February and was to be made captain in March, treated this Lieutenant von Hausen humanely and courteously as soon as he had landed. In all his mentions up to that time Guynemer had been described as a "brilliant chasing pilot"; he was now mentioned as an "incomparable chasing pilot."

* * * * * * * *

Early in April the Storks left Lorraine and went to make their nests on a plateau on the left bank of the Aisne, back of Fismes. New events were in preparation. After the German retreat to the Hindenburg line, the French army in connection with the English army—which was to attack Vimy cliffs (April 9-10, 1917)— was about to undertake that vast offensive operation which, from Soissons to Auberive in Champagne, was to roll like an ocean wave over the slopes of the Chemin des Dames, the hills of Sapigneul and Brimont, and the Moronvillers mountain. Hearts were filled with hope, and the men were inspired by a sacred joy. Their sufferings and their wounds did not prevent the hearts of the soldiers in that spring of 1917 from flowering in sublime sacrifices for the cause of liberty.

As at the battle of the Somme, so at the battle of the Aisne our aerial escadrilles were in close touch with the general staff and the other arms of the service. Their success was no doubt dependent upon the quality of the aeroplanes, and the factory output, and limited by the enemy's power in the air. But though they were unable to achieve the mastery of the air from the very first, they continued obstinately to increase their force, and little by little their successes increased. They had to oppose an enemy who had just accomplished an immense improvement in his aviation corps.

In September, 1916, the German staff, profiting by the lessons of the Somme campaign during which its aviation forces had been so terribly scourged, resolved upon an almost complete reorganization of its aeronautical service. Hindenburg's program arranged for a re-handling of both the direction and the technical services. A decree dating from November, 1916, announced the separation from the other services of the Air Fight Forces (*Luftstreitkräfte*), which were to be placed under a staff officer, the *Kommandeur der Luftstreitkräfte*. This new *Kommandeur*, who was to superintend the building of the machines as well as the training of the pilots, was Lieutenant General von Hoeppner, with Lieutenant Colonel Tjomsen as an assistant. The squadrons, numbering more than 270, were divided into bombing, chasing, patrolling and field escadrilles, these last being entrusted with scouting, photographing, and artillery work, in constant touch with the infantry. Most of these novelties were servilely copied from French aviation. The Germans had borrowed the details of liaison service, as well as those for the regulation of artillery fire, from the French regulations. The commander of the aeronautical section of the Fifth German Army (Verdun) said in a report that "a conscientious aviator was the only reliable inform-ant in action." And his supreme chief, the Kronprinz, commenting upon this sentence, drew the following conclusions:

All this shows once more that through methodical use of infantry aviation, the command can be kept informed of developments through the whole battle. But the necessary condition for fruitful work in the field lies in a previous training carried on with the infantry, machine-guns, artillery, and liaison units. The task of the infantry flyer is apt to be-come more difficult as the weather grows worse, and ground more deeply ploughed up, the enemy more pressing, or our own troops yielding ground. When all these unfavourable circumstances are united, the Infantry Aviator can only be effective if he has perfect training. So he must be in constant contact with the other services, and the Infantry must know him personally. At a pinch he ought to make himself under-stood by the troops, even without any of the usual signals.

But these aeroplanes, while doing this special work, must be protected by patrolling escadrilles. The best protection is afforded by the chasing units, fitted to spread terror and death far afield, or to stop enemy escadrilles bound on a similar errand. Here again, copying the French services, Germany strengthened her chasing escadrilles during the whole winter of 1916-1917, and by the fol-lowing spring she possessed no less than forty. Before the war she had given her attention almost exclusively to heavy aeroplanes.

French types were plagiarized: as the Morane had been altered into the Fokker, the Nieuport became an Albatros. Their one-seated 160 H.P. Albatros, with a Benz or Mercédès fixed engine and two Maxim guns shooting through the propeller, was henceforth the typical chasing machine. However, the powerful two-engine Gothas (520 H.P.) and the Friedrichshafen and A.E.G. (450 H.P.) soon made their appearance in bombing escadrilles.

At the same time, the defensive attitude adopted at the beginning of the Somme campaign was repudiated. The order of the day became strong concentration, likely to secure, at least in one sector, decided superiority in the air, even if other sectors must be left destitute or battle shirked. The flying men were never to be over-worked, so as to be fresh in an emergency. The subordination of aviation to the other services was evidently an inspiration from the French regulation saying:

> The aviation forces shall be always ready to attack, but in perfect subordination to the orders of the commanding officers.

In spite of this *readiness to attack*, the enemy recommended prudence in scouting and patrolling work. The airman was not to engage in a fight without special orders. He seldom cruises by himself, and most often is one of five. To one Boelcke, fond of high altitudes and given to pouncing falcon like on his prey, like Guynemer, there are scores of Richtofens who, under careful protection from other aeroplanes, circle round and round trying to attract the enemy, and unexpectedly getting behind him by a spiral or a loop. It should be said here that the German controlling boards take the pilot's word concerning the number of his victories instead of requiring, as the French do, the evidence of eye witnesses. The high figures generously allowed to a Richtofen or a Werner Voss are less creditable than the strictly controlled record of a Guynemer, a Nungesser, or a Dormé.

The enemy expected in April, 1917, a massive attack from the French air forces in the Aisne, and had taken measures to evade it. An order from the staff of the Seventh Army says that all flying units shall be given the alarm whenever a large number of French aeroplanes are sighted. The German machines must return to camp at once, refusing combat except on equal terms; and balloons must be lowered, or even pulled down to the ground. If, on the contrary, the German machines took the offensive, the order was that, at the hour determined upon, all available machines must rise together to a low altitude, and divide into two distinct fleets, the chasing units flying above the rest. These two fleets must then make for the point of attack, gaining height as they go, and must engage the enemy above the lines with the utmost energy, never giving up the pursuit until they reach the French lines, when the danger from anti-aircraft batteries becomes too great.

From this it is evident that the preference of German Aviation for taking the offensive was not sufficient to induce it to offer battle above the enemy lines, and the tendency of the staff was to group squadrons into overpowering masses. The French had preceded their opponents in the way of technical progress, but the Germans made up for the inferiority, as usual, by method and system. The French were unrivalled for technical improvements, and the training of their pilots. Their new machine, the Spad, was a first-rate instrument, superior in strength, speed, and ease of control to the best Albatros, and the Germans knew that this inferiority must be obviated. All modern battles are thus preceded by technical rivalry. The preparation in factories, week after week, and month after month, ultimately results in living machinery which the staff uses as it pleases.

Living machinery it is, but it is in appearance only that it seems to be independent of man. A battle is a collective work, to which each participant, from the General-in-chief to the road-mender behind the lines, brings his contribution. Colossal though the whole seems, perfect as the enormous machine seems to be, it would not work if there were not behind it a weak man made of poor flesh. A humble gunner, the anonymous defenders of a trench, a pilot who purges the air of the hostile presence, an observer who secures information in good time, some poor soldier who has no idea that his individual action was connected with the great drama, has occasionally brought about wonderful results—as a stone falling into a pool makes its presence felt to the remotest banks.

Amidst the fighters on the Aisne, Guynemer was at his post in the Storks Escadrille. "Alright! They tumble down," he wrote laconically to his family. There were indeed some five tumbling down: on May 25 he had surpassed all that had been done so far in aerial fights, bringing down four German machines in that one day. His notebook states the fact briefly:

8.30.—Downed a two-seater, which lost a wing as it fell and was smashed on the trees 1200 metres NNE. of Corbeny.

8.31.—Another two-seater downed, in flames, above Juvincourt.—With Captain Auger, forced another two-seater to dive down to 600 metres, one kilometre from our lines.

Downed a D.F.W.[22] in flames above Courlandon.

Downed a two-seater in flames between Guignicourt and Condé-sur-Suippes. Dispersed with Captain Auger a squadron of six one-seaters.

Now, his Excellency, Lieutenant General von Hoeppner, *Kommandeur der Luftstreitkräfte*, being interviewed two days later by newspaper men he had summoned for the purpose, told them and through them told Germany and, if possible, the whole world, that the German aeroplanes and the German airmen were unrivalled. he went on to say remarkably apropos:

As for the French aviators, they only engage our men when they are sure of victory. When they have doubts about their own superiority, they prefer to desist rather than take any risks.

This solemn lie the newspaper men repeated at once in their issues of May 28. A few months later one of these same reporters, reverting to the subject of French aviation, took Guynemer himself to task in the *Badische Presse* for August 8, 1917, as follows:

The airman you see flying so high is the famous Guynemer. He is the rival of the most daring German aviators, an *as*, as the French call their champions. He is undoubtedly to be reckoned with, for he handles his machine with absolute

---

22: The D.F.W. (*Deutsche Flugzeug Werke*) is a scouting machine provided with two machine-guns, one shooting through the propeller, the other mounted on a turret aft. It is thirty-nine feet across the wings, and twenty-four in length. One Benz six-cylinder engine of 200/225 H.P. Its speed at an altitude of 3000 metres supposed to be 150 kilometres an hour. One of these machines has been on view at the Invalides since July, 1917.

mastery, and he is an excellent shot. But he only accepts an air fight when every chance is on his side. He flies above the German lines at altitudes between 6000 and 7000 metres, quite out of range of our anti-aircraft artillery. He cannot make any observations, for from that height he sees nothing clearly, not even troops on the march. He is exclusively a chasing flyer bent on destroying our own machines. He has been often successful, though he cannot be compared to our own Richtofen. He is very prudent; always flying, as I said above, at an altitude of at least 6000 metres, he waits till an aeroplane rises from the German lines or appears on its way home. Then he pounces upon it as a falcon might, and opens fire with his machine-gun. When he only wounds the pilot, or if our airman seems to show fight, Guynemer flies back to his own lines at the incredible speed of 250 kilometres an hour, which his very powerful machine makes possible. He never accepts a fair fight. Every man chases as he can.

Every man chases as he can. Quite so. To revert to that 25th of May, the "very prudent" Guynemer, on his morning patrol, met three German aeroplanes flying towards the French lines. They were two-seaters, less nimble, no doubt, than one-seaters, but provided with so much more dangerous arms. Naturally he could not think of attacking them, "not feeling sure of victory," and "always avoiding a risky contest!" Yet he pounced upon his three opponents, who promptly turned back. However, he overtook one, began making evolutions around him, succeeded in getting slightly below him, fired, and with his first volley succeeded in bringing him down in flames north of Corbeny (northeast of Craonne).

The danger for a one-seater is to be surprised from behind. Just as Guynemer veered round, he saw another machine flying after him. He again fired upwards, and the aeroplane fell in flames, like the first, only a few seconds having elapsed between the two fights. Guynemer then returned to camp.

But he was excited by these two fights; his nerves were strained and his will was tense. He soon started again. Towards noon a German machine appeared above the camp itself. How had it been able to get there? This is what the airmen down below were asking themselves. It was useless to chase it, for it would take any of them longer to rise than the German to escape. So they had to content themselves with looking up, some of them searching the sky with binoculars. Everybody was back except Guynemer, when sombody suddenly cried:

"Here comes Guynemer!"

"Then the Boche is done for."

Guynemer, in fact, was coming down upon his prey like lightning, and the instant he was behind and slightly beneath him, he fired. Only one shot from the machine-gun was heard, but the enemy aeroplane was already spinning down, its engine going full speed, and was dashed into the earth at Courlandon near Fismes. The pilot had been shot through the head.

In the afternoon the very prudent Guynemer started for the third time, and towards seven o'clock, above the Guignicourt market gardens (that is to say, in the enemy lines), he brought down another machine in flames.

Very prudent is the last epithet one could have expected to see in connection with the name of Guynemer. For he rarely came home without bullet-holes in his wings or even in his clothes. The Boche, being the Boche, had shown his usual respect for truth and generosity towards an adversary.

Guynemer, when returning to camp after a victory, generally announced his success by making his engine work to some tune. This time the cadence was the tune of the *Lampions*. All the neighbouring aeroplane sheds understood, also the cantonments, parks, depots, dugouts, field hospitals and railway stations; in a word, all the communities scattered behind the lines of an army. This time the motor was singing so insistently that everybody, with faces upturned, concluded that their Guynemer had been "getting them."

In fact, the news was already spreading like wildfire, as news has the mysterious capacity for doing. No, it was not simply one aeroplane he had set ablaze; it was two, one above Corbeny, the other above Juvincourt. And people had hardly realized the wonderful fact before the third machine was seen falling in flames near Fismes. It was seen by hundreds of men who thought it was about to fall upon them, and ran for shelter. Meanwhile, Guynemer's engine was singing.

And for the fourth time it was heard again at twilight. Could it be possible? Had Guynemer really succeeded four times? Four machines brought down in one day by one pilot was what no infantryman, gunner, pioneer, territorial, Anamite or Senegalese had ever seen. And from the stations, field hospitals, dugouts, depots, parks and cantonments, while the setting sun lingered in the sky on this May evening, whoever handled a shovel, a pickaxe or a rifle, whoever laid down rails, unloaded trucks, piled up cases, or broke stones on the road, whoever dressed wounds, gave medicine or carried dead men, whoever worked, rested, ate or drank—whoever was alive, in a word—stepped out, ran, jostled along, arrived at the camp, got helter-skelter over the fences, broke into the sheds, searched the aeroplanes, and called to the mechanicians in their wild desire to see Guynemer. There they were, a whole town of them, knocking at every door and peeping into every tent.

Somebody said: "Guynemer is asleep."

Whereupon, without a word of protest, without a sound, the crowd streamed out and scattered in the darkening fields, threading its way back to the quiet dells behind the lines.

So ended the day of the greatest aerial victory.

CHAPTER 2

A Visit to Guynemer

Sunday, June 3, 1917. Today, the first Sunday of June, the women from the neighbouring villages came to visit the camp. Nobody is allowed to enter, but from the road you can see the machines start or land. The day was glorious, and the broad sun transfiguring these French landscapes, with their elongated valleys, their wooded ranges of hills, and generally harmonious lines suggested Greece, and one looked around for the colonnades of temples.

Beyond the rolling country rose the Aisne cliffs, where the fighting was incessant, though its roar was scarcely perceived.

Why had these villages been attracted to this particular camp? Because they knew that here, in default of Greek temples, were young gods. They wanted to see Guynemer.

The news had flown on rapid wings from hamlet to hamlet, from farm to farm, of what had happened on the 25th, and on the next day Guynemer had been almost equally successful.

Several aviators had already landed, men with famous names, but the public cannot be expected to remember them all. Finally an aeroplane descended in graceful spirals, landing softly and rolling along close to the railings.

"Guynemer!"

But the pilot, unconscious of the worshiping crowd, took off his helmet, disclosed a frowning face, and began discontentedly to examine his gun. Twice that day it had jammed, saving two Germans. Guynemer was like the painters of old who, by grinding their colours themselves, insured the duration of their works. He resented not being able to make all his weapons himself, his engine, his Vickers, and his bullets. At length he seemed willing to leave his machine, and pulled off his heavy war accoutrement, which revealed a tall, flexible young man. As he rapidly approached his tent, his every motion watched by the onlookers, a private turned on him a small camera, with a beseeching—

"You'll permit me, *mon capitaine?*"

"Yes, but quick."

He was cross and impatient, and as he stopped he noticed all the eyes of the women watching him ecstatically. He made a despairing gesture. His frown deepened, his figure stiffened, and the snapshot was another failure.

Hardly any of his portraits are like him. Does the fact that he was tall and spare, almost beardless, with an amber-coloured, oval face and a regular profile, and raven-hair brushed backwards, give any idea of the force that was in him? If his eyes, dark with golden reflections, could have been painted, they might no doubt have given a more accurate notion of him: his capacity for surveying all space, and his prompt decision, were visible in them, as well as his carefulness and his courage. Their glance was so direct, almost brutal, that it could be felt, so to speak, physically; and yet it could suddenly express a cheerful, boyish nature, or disclose his close attention to the technical problems which everlastingly engrossed his mind.

Guynemer was very different from Navarre, with his powerful profile and broad chest like an eagle in repose, and different from Nungesser, the Nungesser before his wounds had so devastated his body that a medical board wanted to declare him unfit, a decision which he heroically resisted, adding to his thirty victories another triumph over physical disability. Guynemer differed from them mentally, too, possessing neither their instinct nor their intuitiveness. These he replaced with scientific accuracy based on study, by a passion for flying, by method allied to fervour, by violent logic. His power was nervous and almost electric. The vicinity of danger drew sparks from him.

His most daring exploits were prepared by meditation beforehand, and he never indulged in recklessness without having pondered and calculated. His action was so swift that it might seem instinctive, but under appearances the reasoning element was always present.

It was now late, but he was willing to talk to us about that wonderful 25th of May, for he had no objection to talking about his enemy-chasing; on the contrary, he would tell us details with the same amusement as if he related lucky plays at poker, and with the same knowing ways. There was not the least shade of affectation or of posing in his narrative, but he talked with the simplicity of a child. He told us that his third encounter had been the most enjoyable. He was coming back to lunch, had seen the impudent German soaring above the camp, had fired, and the man had gone down dead. After this exceedingly brief account he laughed as usual, a fresh laugh like a girl's, and his eyes closed. He said he was sleepy; he had been out twice, and before he went again he wanted a little rest.

* * * * * * * *

I remember how bustling the camp looked! It was half-past six, and the weather was wonderful, with not a cloud in the sky, for some floating white flakes in the blue could not be called clouds. But these white flakes began to multiply; they were, in fact, an enemy patrol, which had succeeded in crossing the lines and was now above us. We counted two, three, four machines, which the sparks of our exploding shells promptly surrounded, while three French Spads rose at full speed to meet them.

As we stood watching and wondering if the enemy would accept the fight, Guynemer suddenly appeared. He had been called, and now he and his comrades, Captain Auger and Lieutenant Raymond, came running to their machines. I watched Guynemer as he was being put into his leather suit. His whole soul was in his eyes, which glared at one moving point in space as if they themselves could shoot. Three of the German machines had already turned back, but the remaining one went on, insolently counting on his own power and speed. I shall never forget Guynemer, his face lifted, his eyes illuminated as if hypnotized by this point in space, his figure upright and stiffened like an arrow waiting to be released by the bow. Before pulling down his helmet he gave the order:

"Straight at him."

The engines snorted and snored, the propellers began to move, the machines rolled along, and suddenly were seen climbing almost vertically. Up above the fight was beginning, and it seemed as if the

129

three starting aeroplanes could never reach in time the altitude of four or five thousand metres at which it was taking place.

The attacking Spad was obviously trying to get its opponent within firing range, but the German was a first-rate pilot and dodged without losing height, banking, looping, taking advantage of the Frenchman's dead angles, and striving to get him under his machine-gun. Round and round the two aeroplanes circled, when suddenly the German bolted in the direction of the Aisne cliffs. But the Spad partly caught up with him and the aerial circling began anew, while two other Spads appeared—a pack after a deer. The German cleverly took advantage now of the sun, now of the evening vapours, but he was within range, and the tack-tack of a machine-gun was heard. Guynemer and the other two were coming nearer, when the Spad dropped beneath its adversary and fired upwards. The German plunged, and we expected would sink, but he righted himself and was off in an instant. However, this was Guynemer's chance: three shots, not more, from his gun, and the German aeroplane crashed down somewhere near Muizon, on the banks of the Vesle.[23]

One after another, the victorious birds came back to cover from every part of the violet and rosy sky. But joy over their success must show itself, and they indulged in all the fanciful caprioles of acrobatic aviation, spinning down in quick spirals, turning somersaults, looping or plunging in a glorious sky-dance. Last of these young gods, Guynemer landed after one final circle, and took off his helmet, offering to the setting sun his illuminated face, still full of the spirit of battle.

23: This victory was not put down to Guynemer's account, because another airman had shot first—which gives an idea of the French controlling board's severity.

CHAPTER 3

Guynemer in Camp

On the Somme Guynemer was one of the great French champions; on the Aisne he became their king. No enemy could resist him, and his daring appeared without bounds. On May 27 he attacked alone a squadron of six two-seaters above Auberive at an altitude of 5000 metres, and compelled them to go down to an altitude of 3600 metres. Before landing, he pounced on another group of eight, scattering them and bringing down one, completely smashed, with its fuselage linen in rags, among the shell-holes in a field. He was like the Cid Campeador, to whom the Sheik Jabias said:

> ... Vous éclatiez, avec des rayons jusqu'aux cieux,
> Dans une préséance éblouissante aux yeux;
> Vous marchiez, entouré d'un ordre de bataille;
> Aucun sommet n'était trop haut pour votre taille,
> Et vous étiez un fils d'une telle fierté
> Que les aigles volaient tous de votre côté....

His feats exceeded all hopes, and his appearance in the sky fairly frightened the enemy. On June 5, after bringing down an Albatros east of Berry-au-Bac, he chased to the east of Rheims a D.F.W., which had previously been attacked by other Spads. Guynemer's notebook says:

> My nose was right on him when my machine-gun jammed. But just then the observer raised his hands. I beckoned to him several times to veer towards our lines, but noticing that he was making straight for his own, I went back to my gun, which now worked, and fired a volley of fifteen (at 2200 altitude). Immediately the machine upset, throwing the observer overboard, and sank on Berru forest.

131

However, Guynemer's day's work was not done to his satisfaction after these two victories (his forty-fourth and forty-fifth): he attacked a group of three, and later on a group of four, and came back with bullets in his machine.

Meanwhile he had been made, on June 11, 1917, an Officer of the Legion of Honour with the following citation:

A remarkable officer, a daring and dexterous chaser. Has been of exceptional service to the country both by the number of his victories and by the daily example of his never-flagging courage and constantly increasing mastery. Careless of danger, he has become, by the infallibility of his methods, the most formidable opponent of German flyers. On May 25 achieved unparalleled success, bringing down two machines in one minute, and two more in the course of the same day. By these exploits has contributed to maintaining the courage and enthusiasm of the men who, from the trenches, have witnessed his triumphs. Forty-five machines brought down; twenty citations; twice wounded.

This document, eloquent and accurate and tracing facts to their causes, praises in Guynemer at the same time will-power, courage, and the contagion of example. Guynemer loved the last sentence, because it associated with his fights their daily witnesses, the infantrymen in the trenches.

The badge of an Officer in the Legion of Honour was given to him at the aviation camp on July 5 by General Franchet d'Esperey, in command of the Northern Armies. But this solemn ceremony had not prevented Guynemer from flying twice, the first time for two hours, the second flight one hour, on a new machine from which he expected wonders. He attacked three D.F.W.'s, and had to land with five bullets in his engine and radiator.

His new decoration was given him at four o'clock on a beautiful summer afternoon. Guynemer's comrades were present, of course, and as pleased as if the function had concerned themselves. The 11th Company of the 82nd Regiment of Infantry took its station opposite the imposing row of squadron machines, sixty in number, which stood there like race horses as if to take part in the fete. Guynemer's well-known aeroplane, the *Vieux-Charles*, was the fifth to the left, its master having required its presence, though it had been injured that very day. In front of the aviation and regimental flags the young aviator stood by himself in his black *vareuse*, looking slight and pale, but upright, with eyes sparkling. At a little distance a few civilians—his own people, whom the general had invited—watched the proceedings.

General Franchet d'Esperey appeared, a robust, energetic man, and the following scene, described by one of the trench papers—the *Brise d'entonnoirs* of the 82nd Infantry—took place:

> The general stopped before the young hero and eyed him with evident pleasure; then he proclaimed him a gallant soldier, touched his two shoulders with his sword, as they did to champions of past ages, pinned the rosette on his coat, and embraced him. Then to the stirring tune of *Sambre-et-Meuse* the band and the soldiers marched in front of the new officer who, the ceremony now being over, joined his relatives some distance away.

General d'Esperey, looking over Guynemer's *Vieux-Charles*, noticed the damaged parts.

"How comes it that your foot was not injured?" he asked, pointing to one of the bullet-holes.

"I had just removed it, *mon général*," said Guynemer, with his usual simplicity.

None of the airmen with whom Guynemer shared his joy ever forgot that afternoon of July 5, 1917. The summer sun, the serene beauty of the hills bordering the Aisne, the distant bass of the battle, lent to the scene an enchanting but solemn interest. Tragic memories were in the minds of all the bystanders, and great names were on their lips—the names of retiring, noble, hard-working Dormé, reported missing on May 25, and of Captain Lecour-Grandmaison, creator of the three-seaters, who, on one of these machines, brought down five Germans, but was killed in a combat on May 10 and brought back to camp dead by a surviving comrade. Guynemer's red rosette meant glory to the great chasers, to wounded Heurtaux, to Ménard and Deullin, to Auger, Fonck, Jailler, Guérin, Baudouin, and all their comrades! And it meant glory to the pilots and observers who, always together in the discharge of duty, are not infrequently together in meeting death: to Lieutenant Fressagues, pilot, and sous-lieutenant Bouvard, observer, who once fought seven Germans and managed to bring one down; to Lieutenant Floret and Lieutenant Homo, who, placed in similar circumstances, set two machines on fire; to Lieutenant Viguier who, on April 18, had the pluck to come down to twenty-five metres above the enemy's lines and calmly make his observations; and to so many others who did their duty with the same daring, intelligence, and conscientiousness, to the hundreds of more humble airmen who, while the infantry says the sanguinary mass, throw down from above, like the chorister boys in the *corpus Christi* procession, the red roses of epics!

The whole Storks Escadrille had received from General Duchêne the following citation:

Escadrille No. 3. Commander: Captain Heurtaux. A brilliant chasing escadrille which for the past two years has fought in every sector of the front with wonderful spirit and admirable self-sacrifice. The squadron has just taken part in the Lorraine and Champagne operations, and during this period its members have destroyed fifty-three German machines which, added to others previously brought down, makes a total of one hundred and twenty-eight certainly demolished, and one hundred and thirty-two partly disabled.

This battle on the Aisne, with its famous climax at the Chemin des Dames, began to slacken in July; and it was decided that the chasing squadrons, including the Storks, should be transferred to one of the British sectors where another offensive was being prepared. But before leaving the Fismes or Rheims district, Guynemer was active. He had not been given his new rank in the Legion of Honour to be idle: that was not his way. On the contrary, his habit was to show, after receiving a distinction as well as before, that he was worthy of it. On July 6 he engaged five two-seaters, and brought down one in flames. The next day his notebook records two more victories:

Attacked with Adjutant Bozon-Verduraz, four Albatros one-seaters, above Brimont. Downed one in flames north of Villers-Franqueux, in our own lines. Attacked a D.F.W. which spun down in our lines at Moussy.

These victories, his forty-sixth, forty-seventh, and forty-eighth, were his farewell to the Aisne. But these excessive exertions brought on nervous fatigue. The escadrille had only just reached its new station, when Guynemer had to go into hospital, whence he wrote his father on July 18 as follows:

Dear Father:
Knocked out again. Hospital. But this time I'm flourishing. No more wooden barracks, but a farmhouse right in the fields. I have a room all to myself. Quite correct: I downed three Fritzes, one ablaze, and the next day again great sport: mistook four Boches for Frenchmen. At first fought three of them, then one alone at 3200 to 800 metres. He took fire. They will have to wait till the earth dries so they can dig him out. An hour later a two-seater turned up at 5500. He blundered, and fell straight down on a 75, which died of the shock. But so did the passenger. The pilot was simply a bit excited, for which he couldn't be blamed. His machine had not plunged, but came down slowly, with its nose twirling, and I got his two guns intact....

The *toubib* (doctor) says I shall be on my feet in three or four days. Don't see many Boches just now, but that won't last. I read in a newspaper that I had been mobbed in a friendly manner in Paris. I must be ubiquitous without knowing it. Modern science brings about marvels, modern journalism also.

Raymond has two strings (officer's stripes) and the cross of the Legion. Please congratulate him.

Goodnight, father.

Georges

P.S. I, who get seasick over nothing at all, have just been out to sea for the first time. The water was very rough, especially for a little motor-boat, but I smiled serenely through it all. Wasn't I proud!...

In fact, some newspaper had announced that Guynemer would carry the aviation flag in the parade of the 14th of July in Paris, and this was enough to persuade the crowd that some other airman was Guynemer. Indeed, there had been talk of sending him to Paris on that solemn occasion, but he had declined. He loved glory, but hated show, and he had followed his squadron to Flanders, where he had taken to his bed.

The foregoing letter bears Guynemer's mark unmistakably. The son of rich parents rejoicing over having a room to himself, after having renounced all comfort from the very first day of his enlistment, and willing to begin as *garçon d'aérodrome*; the joke about the German aeroplane sunk so deep in the wet ground that it would have to be dug out, and the surprise of the pilot; the delight over Raymond's promotion; the amusing allusion to sea-sickness by the man who had no equal in air navigation, are all characteristic details.

Sheik Jabias thus sums up his impressions after visiting the Cid in his camp:

Vous dominiez tout, grand, sans chef, sans joug, sans digue,
Absolu, lance au poing, panache, au front....

And that Cid had never fought up in the air.

CHAPTER 4

Guynemer in His Father's House

To quote him once more, Sheik Jabias, after being dazzled by the Cid in his camp, is supposed to see him in his father's castle at Bivar, doing more humble work.

> ...*Que s'est-il donc passé? Quel est cet équipage?*
> *J'arrive, et je vous trouve en veste, comme un page,*
> *Dehors, bras nus, nu-tête, et si petit garcon*
> *Que vous avez en main l'auge et le caveçon,*
> *Et faisant ce qu'il sied aux écuyers de faire,*
> *—Cheick, dit le Cid, je suis maintenant chez mon père.*

Those who never saw Guynemer at his father's at Compiègne cannot know him well. Of course, even in camp he was the best of comrades, full of his work, but always ready to enjoy somebody else's success, and speaking about his own as if it were billiards or bridge. His renown had not intoxicated him, and he would have been quite unconscious of it had he not sometimes felt that unresponsiveness on the part of others which is the price of glory: anything like jealousy hurt him as if it had been his first discovery of evil. In Kipling's *Jungle Book*, Mowgli, the man cub, noticing that the Jungle hates him, feels his eyes and is frightened at finding them wet. "What is this, Bagheera?" he asks of his friend the panther. "Oh, nothing; only tears," answers Bagheera, who had lived among men.

One who, on occasion, told Guynemer *not to mind* knows how deep was his sensitiveness, not to the presence of real hostility, which he fortunately never encountered, but even to an obscure germ of jealousy. The moment he felt this he shrank into himself. His native exuberance only displayed itself under the influence of sympathy.

Friendship among airmen is manly and almost rough, not caring for formulas or appearances, but proving itself by deeds. To these men the games of war are astonishingly like school games, and are spoken of as if they were nothing else. When a comrade has not come back, and dinner has to begin without him, no show of sorrow is tolerated: only these young men's hearts feel the absence of a friend, and the casual visitor, not knowing, might take them for sporting men, lively and jolly.

Guynemer was living his life in perfect confidence, feeling no personal ambition, not inclined to enjoy honours more than work, ignoring all affectation or attitudinizing, never politic, and naturally unconscious of his own simplicity. Yet he loved and adored what we call glory, and would tell anybody of his successes, even of his decorations, with a childlike certitude that these things must delight others as much as himself. His French honours were of course his great pride, but he highly appreciated those which he had received from allied governments, too: the Distinguished Service order, the Cross of St. George, the Cross of Leopold, the Belgian war medal, Serbian and Montenegrin orders, etc. All these ribbons made a bright show, and although he generally wore only the rosette of the Legion of Honour, he would sometimes deck himself out in them all, or carry them in his pocket and occasionally empty them out on a table, as at school he used to tumble out the untidy contents of his desk in search of his task. When he went to Paris to see to his machines, he first secured a room at the Hôtel Edouard VII, and immediately posted to the Buc works. When he had time he would invite himself to dinner at the house of his schoolmate at the Collège Stanislas, Lieutenant Constantin; this officer writes:

> Every time he came some new exploit or a new decoration had been added to his list. He never wore all his medals, his 'village-band banner,' as he amusingly called them; but when people asked to see them, he immediately searched his pockets and produced the whole disorderly lot. When he became officer in the Legion, he appeared at my mother's quite radiant, so that she asked him the reason of this unusual joy. '*Regardez bien, madame*, there is something new.' The new thing which my mother discovered was a tiny rosette ornamenting his red ribbon.

This rosette was so very small that nobody noticed it, and Guynemer felt that he must complain to the shop man at the Palais Royal who had sold it to him.

"Give me a larger one, a huge one," he said; "nobody sees this."

****

The tradesman spread a number of rosettes on his counter, but Guynemer only took back again the one of which he had complained, and went out laughing as if the whole thing had been a good joke.

His officer's stripes gave him as much pleasure as his decorations. Every time he was promoted, he wanted his stripes sewn on, not in a day or an hour, or even five minutes, but immediately. He received his captain's commission the same day he had been given the Distinguished Service order, and he promptly went to see his friend, Captain de la Tour, who was wounded in the hospital at Nancy. This officer had lost three brothers in action, and loved Guynemer as if he had been another younger brother. Indeed, Guynemer said later that La Tour loved him more than any other did.

"Don't you see any change in me?" Guynemer asked.

"No, you're just as usual."

"No, there's a change!"

"Oh, I see; you mean your English order; it does look well."

"There's something else. Look closer."

La Tour at last discovered the three stripes on the cap and sleeves.

"What! Are you a captain?"

"Yes, a captain," and Guynemer laughed his boyish laugh.— *This kid a captain! So I am not an impressive captain, then? I haven't run risks enough to be a captain, probably!*—His laugh said all this.

Lieutenant Constantin also says in his notes:

Guynemer disliked walking about Paris, because people recognized him. When he saw them turn to look at him, he would grumble at the curse of having a face that was public property. So he preferred waiting for evening, and then drove his little white car up the Champs Elysées to the Bois. He enjoyed this peaceful recreation thoroughly, and forgot the excitement of his life at the front. Memories of our boyhood days came back to him, and he dwelt on them with delight: 'Do you remember one day in *seconde* when we quarrelled and fought like madmen? You made such a mark on my arm that it is there yet.' He did not mind, but I was ashamed of having been such a young brute. Another day, in May, 1917, coming home on leave I met Georges just as he stepped out of his hotel, and as I had just been mentioned in dispatches I told him about it. Immediately he dragged me into a shop, bought a *croix de guerre*, pinned it on my *vareuse*, and hugged me before everybody.

Guynemer had a genius for graciousness, and his imagination was inexhaustible when he wished to please, but his temper was hot and quick. One day he had left his motor at the door of the hotel, and some practical joker thought it clever to leave a note in the car with this inscription in large letters:

AVIATORS TO THE FRONT!

Guynemer did not take the joke at all, and was boiling with rage. His complete freedom from conceit has often been remarked. At a luncheon given in his honour by the well-known deputy, Captain Lasies, he would not say a word about himself, but extolled his comrades until somebody said: "You are really modesty itself."

Whereupon another guest asked: "Could you imagine him bragging?"

Guynemer was delighted, and when the party broke up he went out with the gentleman who had said this and thanked him warmly. "Don't you see how little they understand? I don't say I am modest, but if I weren't I would be a fool, and I should not like to be that. I know quite well that just now some of us are getting so much admiration and so many honours that one may get more than one's share. Whereas the men in the trenches—how different it is with them!"[24]

But it was inevitable that he should be lionized. People came to him with albums and pictures. He wrote to his father that a Madame de B. wanted something, just one sentence, in an album which was to be sold in America. "I am to be alongside the Generalissimo. What on earth can I write?"

24: *Journal des Débats* for September 26, 1917.

An American lady who was also a guest at the Hôtel Edouard VII wanted to have at any price some souvenir of the young hero. She ordered her maid to bring away an old glove of Guynemer's which was lying on a chest of drawers, and replace it by a magnificent bouquet. "This lady put me in a nice dilemma," Guynemer explained, "as it was Sunday and there was no way of getting any more gloves."[25]

He had no affectation, least of all the kind that pretends to be ignorant of one's own popularity; but surely he cared little for popularity. Here again he puts us in mind of a medieval poem. In *Gilbert de Metz*, one of our oldest epics, the daughter of Anséis is described seated at the window, "fresh, slim, and white as a lily" when two knights, Garin and his cousin Gilbert, happen to ride near.

"Look up, cousin Gilbert," says Garin, "look. By our lady, what a handsome dame!"

"Oh," answers Gilbert, "what a handsome creature my steed is! I never saw anything so lovely as this maiden with her fair skin and dark eyes. I never knew any steed that could compare with mine."

And so on, while Gilbert still refuses to look up at the beautiful daughter of Anséis. Also in *Girard de Viane*, Charlemagne, holding his court at the palace of Vienne, has just placed the hand of the lovely Aude in that of his nephew Roland. Both the girl and the great soldier are silent and blushing while the date of the wedding is being discussed, when a messenger suddenly rushes in:

"The Saracens are in France! War! war!" shout the bystanders.

Then without a word Roland drops the white hand of the girl, springs to arms, and is gone. So Guynemer would have praised his Nieuport or his Spad as Gilbert praised his steed, and *belle Aude* herself could not have kept him away from the fight.

One day his father felt doubts about the capacity of such a young man to resist the intoxication of so much flattery from men and women.

"Don't worry," Guynemer answered, "I am watching my nerves as an acrobat watches his muscles. I have chosen my own mission, and I must fulfil it."

After his death, one of his friends, the one who spoke to him last, told me:

25: Anecdote related in the *Figaro* for September 29, 1917.

COMBAT

He used to put aside heaps of flattering letters which he did not even read. 'Read them if you like,' he said to me, and I destroyed them. He only read letters from children, school-boys and soldiers.

In *L'Aiglon* Prokesch brings the mail to the Prince Imperial, and handing him letters from women, he says: "*Voilà Ce que c'est d'avoir l'auréole fatale.*"

As soon as Prokesch begins to read them, the Prince stops him with the words: "*Je déchire.*"

Even when a woman whom he has nicknamed "Little Spring"—"because the water sleeping in her eyes or purling in her voice has often cooled his fever"—announces her departure, hoping he may detain her, he lets her go, whispering again like a refrain, "*Je déchire.*"

Did Guynemer deal with hearts as he dealt with the besieging letters, or as the falcon of St. Jean l'Hospitalier dealt with birds?—No "Little Spring," had her voice been ever so rill-like, could have detained him when a sunny morning invited him skywards.

* * * * * * * *

Safe from the admiring public, Guynemer would relax and breathe freely with his people at Compiègne, where he became once more a lively, noisy, indulged, but coaxing and charming boy, except when absorbed in work, from which nothing could distract him. He spent hours in pasting and classifying the snapshots he took of his enemies just before pulling the trigger of his machine-gun and bringing them down. One of his greatest pleasures when on leave was to arrange and show these photographs.

His eyes, which saw everything, were keen to detect the least changes in the arrangement of his home, even when mere knick-knacks had been moved about. At each visit he found the house ornamented with some new trophy of his exploits. He was delighted to find that a miniature barkentine, which he had built with corks, paper, and thread when he was seven years old, still stood on his mother's mantelpiece. Even at that age his powers of observation had been evident, and he had forgotten no detail of sails or rigging.

He had taken again so naturally his old place in the family circle that his mother forgot once and called the tall, famous young man by his old familiar name, "*Bébé*." She quickly corrected herself, but he said:

"I am always that to you, Mother."

"I was happier when you were little," she observed.

"I hope you are not vexed with me, Mother."

"Vexed for what?"

"For having grown up."

He was naturally full of the one subject that interested him, aeroplanes and chasing, and he would go round the house collecting audiences. Strange bits of narration could be overheard from different rooms as he held forth:

"Then I *embusqued* myself became a slacker...."

"What!"

"Oh! I *embusqued* myself behind a cloud."

Or, "The light dazzled me, so I hid the sun with my wing."

He never forgot his sisters' birthdays, but he could not always give them the present he preferred. "Sorry I could not present you with a Boche."

He was hardly different when his mother received company: he was never seen to play the great man. Only on one subject he always and instantly became serious, namely, when the future was mentioned. "Do not let us make any plans," he would say.

* * * * * * * *

A page from one of my own notebooks will help to show Guynemer as I used to see him in his home.

Wednesday, June 27, 1917.—Compiègne. Called on the Guynemers. He is fascination itself with his "goddess on the clouds" gait—as if he remembered when walking that he could also fly—with his incomparable eyes, his perpetual movement, his interior electricity, his admixture of elegance and ardour, and with that impulse of his whole being towards one object which suggests the antique runner, even when he is for an instant in repose. His parents and sisters do not miss a single gesture, a single motion he makes. They drink in his every word, and his life seems to absorb them. His laugh echoes in their souls. They believe in him, are sure of him, sure of his future, and that all will be well. Noticing this certitude, whether real or assumed, I could not help stealing a glance at the frail god of aviation, made like the delicate statuettes that we dread breaking. He talks passionately, as usual, of his aerial fights. But just now one thought seems to supersede every other. He is expecting a new machine, a magic machine which he planned long ago, found difficult to get built, and with which he must do more damage than ever.

Then he showed us his photographs with the white blotches of bursting shells, or the gray wings of German aeroplanes. One of these is seen as it falls in flames, the pilot falling, too, some distance away from it. Thus the victim was registered, and the memory of it made him happy.

I swallowed a question I was going to ask: What about yourself—some day? because he looked so full of life that the notion of death could never present itself to him. But he seemed to have read my thoughts, for he said:

"You have plenty of time in the air, except when you fight, and then you have no time at all. I've been brought down six times, and I always had plenty of time to realize what was happening." And he laughed his clear, boyish laugh.

As a matter of fact, he has been incredibly lucky. In one fight he was hit three times, and each time the bullet was deadened by some unexpected obstacle.

Finally I was shown photographs of himself, chronologically arranged. Needless to say, it was not he who showed them. There was the half-nude baby, with eyes already sparkling and eager, then the schoolboy with the fine carriage of the head, then the lad fresh from school with a singularly calm expression, and well filled-out cheeks. A little later the expression appeared more mature and tense, though still ingenuous. Later again there was a decidedly stern look, with the face less oval and thinner. The rough fingers of war had chiselled this face, and sharpened and strengthened it. I looked from the picture to him, and I realized that, compared to his former pictures, his expression had now indeed acquired something terrible. But just then he laughed, and the laughter conjured away all fantasies.

CHAPTER 5

The Magic Machine

As a tiny boy who had invented an enchanted bed for his sisters' dolls, as a boy who, at Collège Stanislas, had rigged up a telephone to send messages to the last forms in the schoolroom, or manufactured miniature aeroplanes, as a recruit who, at Pau, had gladly accepted the work of cleaning, burnishing, and overhauling engines, Guynemer had always shown a passion for mechanics. Becoming a pilot, and later on a chaser, he exhibited in the study and perfecting of his aeroplanes the same enthusiasm and perseverance as in his flights. He was everlastingly calling for swifter or more powerful machines, and not only strove to communicate his own fervour to technicians, but went into minute details, suggested improvements, and whenever he had a chance visited the workshops and assisted at trials. Such trials are sometimes dangerous. One of his friends, Edouard de Layens, was killed in this kind of accident, and Guynemer was enraged that a gallant airman should perish otherwise than in battle. He was in reality an inventor, though this statement may cause surprise, and though it may not be wise at present to bear it out by facts.

Every part of his machine or of his gun was familiar to him. He had handled them all, taking them apart and putting them together again. There are practical improvements in modern aeroplanes which would not be there had it not been for him. And there is a "Guynemer visor."

Confidence and authoritativeness had not come to him along with glory, for from the first he talked as one engrossed by his ideas, and it is because he was thus engrossed that he found persuasive words to bring others round to his views. But, naturally enough, he had not at first the prestige which he possessed when he became Captain Guynemer, had high rank in the Legion of Honour, and enjoyed world-wide fame. In his 'prentice days when, in workshops or in the presence of well-known builders, he would make confident statements, inveigh against errors, or demand modifications, people thought him flippant and saucy. Once somebody called him a raw lad. The answer came with crushing rapidity: "When you blunder, raw lads like myself pay for your mistakes."

It must be admitted that, like most people brought up with wealth, he was apt to be unduly impatient. Delays or objections irritated him. He wanted to force his will upon Time, which never admits compulsion, and tried to over-ride obstacles. His peculiar fascination gradually won its way even in workshops, and his appearance there was greeted with acclamation, not only because the men were curious to see him, but because they were in sympathy with him and had put his ideas to a successful test. The workmen liked to see him sit in a half-finished machine, and explain in his short, decisive style what he wanted and what was sure to give superiority to French aviation. The men stopped work, came round, and listened eagerly. This, too, was a triumph for him. What he told them on such occasions he had probably whispered to himself many times before when, on rainy days, he would sit in his aeroplane under the hangar, and think and talk to himself, while strangers wondered if he was not crazy.

However, he had made friends with well-known engineers, especially Major Garnier of Puteaux and M. Béchereau of the Spad works. These two, instead of dismissing him as a snappish airman continually at variance with the builder, took his inventions seriously and strove to meet his requirements. When M. Béchereau, after long delays, was at last decorated for his eminent services, the Secretary of Aeronautics, M. Daniel Vincent, came to the works and was going to place the medal and red ribbon on the engineer's breast, when he saw Guynemer standing near. He graciously handed the medal over to the airman, saying:

"Give M Béchereau his decoration; it is only fair you should."

In September, 1916, Guynemer had tried at the front one of the first two Spads. On the 8th he wrote to M. Béchereau:

Well, the Spad has had her *baptême du feu*. The others were six: an Aviatik at 2800, an L.V.G. at 2900, and four Rumplers jostling one another with barely 25 metres in between at 3000 metres. When the four saw me coming (at 1800 on the speedometer) they no doubt took me for a meteorite and funked, and when they got over it and back to their shooting (fine popping, though) it was too late. My gun never jammed once.

Here he went into technicalities about his new machine-gun, but further on reverted to the Spad:

She loops wonderfully. Her spin is a bit lazy and irregular, but deliciously soft.

The letter concludes with many suggestions for minor improvements. His correspondence with M. Béchereau was entirely devoted to a study of aeroplanes: he never wandered from the subject. Thus he collaborated with the engineer by constantly communicating to him the results of his experience. His machine-gun was the great difficulty. On October 21, 1916 he wrote:

Yesterday five Boches, three of them above our lines, came within ten metres of the muzzle of my gun, and impossible to shoot. Four days ago I had to let two others get away. Sickening.... The weather is wonderful. Perhaps the gun will work now.

In fact, a few days later he wrote exultingly, having discovered that the jamming was due to cold and having found an ingenious remedy.

November 4, 1916. Day before yesterday I bagged a Fokker one-seater biplane. It was two metres off, but as it tumbled into a group of our Nieuports, the controlling board would not give the victory to anybody. Yesterday got an Aviatik ten metres off; passenger shot dead by the first bullet; the plane, all in rags, went down in slow spirals and must have been knocked flat somewhere near Berlincourt. Heurtaux, who had seen it beginning to fall, brought one down himself ten minutes later, like a regular ball.

On November 18 next, after going into particulars concerning his engine which he wanted made stronger, he told M. Béchereau of his 21st and 22nd victories:

As for the 21st, it was a one-seater I murdered as it twirled in elegant spirals down to its own landing ground. No. 22 was a 220 H.P., one of three above our lines. I came upon it unawares in a somersault. Passenger stood up, but fell down again in his seat before even setting his gun going. I put some two hundred or two hundred and fifty bullets into him twenty metres away from me. He had taken an invariable angle of 45° on the first volley. When I let him go, Adjutant Bucquet took him in hand—which would have helped if he hadn't already been as full of holes as a strainer. He kept his angle of 45° till about 500 metres, when he adopted the vertical, and blazed up on crashing to the ground....

The Spad ravished him. It was the heyday of wonderful flights on the Somme. Yet he wanted something even better; but before pestering M. Béchereau he began with an inspiring narrative.

December 28, 1916. I can't grumble; yet yesterday I missed my camera badly. I had a high-class round with an Albatros, a fine, clever fellow, between two and ten metres away from me. We only exchanged fifteen shots, and he snapped my right fore-cable—just a few threads still held—while I shot him in the small of his back. A fine spill! (No. 25).

Now, to speak of serious things, I must tell you that the Spad 150 H.P. is not much ahead of the Halberstadt. The latter is not faster, I admit, but it climbs so much more quickly that it amounts to the same thing. However, our latest model knocks them all out....

The letter adds only some recommendations as to the necessity for more speed and a better propeller.

But much more important improvements were already filling his mind. He had conceived plans for a magic aeroplane that would simply annihilate the enemy, and as he would doggedly carry on a fight, so he ruminated, begged, and urged until his idea was realized. But he was forced to practice exhausting perseverance, and on several occasions the lack of comprehension or sympathy which he encountered infuriated him. Yet he never gave up. It was not his way in a workshop, any more than in the air; and when, after some ten months' struggling, trying, and frequent beginning over again, he saw himself at last in possession of the wonderful machine, he rejoiced as a warrior may after forging his own weapons.

In January, 1917, he wrote to M. Béchereau urging him to make all dispatch:

> Spring will soon be here, and the Germans are working like niggers. If we go to sleep, it will be '*couic*' for us.

Henceforth his correspondence, sometimes rather dictatorial, with the engineer was entirely devoted to the magic aeroplane,—its size, controls, wing-tips, tank, weight, etc. The margins of his letters were covered with drawings, and every detail was minutely discussed. In February he wrote to his father as if he had been a builder:

> My machine surpasses all expectations, and will soon be at work. In Paris I go to bed early and rise ditto, spending all day at Spad's. I have no other thought or occupation. It is a fixed idea, and if it goes on I shall become a perfect idiot. When peace is signed, let nobody dare to mention a weapon of any kind in my presence for six months.

He thought himself within reach of his goal; but unexpected obstacles would come in his way, and it was not till July 5, 1917—the same day on which he received the rosette of the Legion of Honour from General Franchet d'Esperey at the Aisne Aviation Camp—that he could at last try the long-dreamed-of, long-hoped-for aeroplane. But in a fight against three D.F.W.'s, the splendid new machine got riddled with bullets, he had to land, and everything had to be begun over again. But Guynemer was not afraid of beginning over again, and in fact he was to give the aeroplane another chance in Flanders, and to see all his expectations fulfilled. The 49th, 50th, 51st and 52nd victories of Guynemer were due to the magic aeroplane.

He managed to impose his will on matter, and on those who adapt it to the warlike conceptions of man, as he imposed it on the enemy. Then, spreading out his wings on high, he might well think himself invincible.

The Ascension

CHAPTER 1

The Battle of Flanders

After the battle on the Aisne Georges Guynemer was ordered to
Flanders, but he had to take to his bed as soon as he arrived (July,
1917) and only left the hospital on the 20th. He then repaired to
the new aviation camp outside Dunkirk, which at that time consisted of a few rows of tents near the seaside. He was to take part in
the contemplated offensive, on his own magic aeroplane—which
he brought from Fismes on the 23rd—for the Storks Escadrille
had been incorporated into a fighting unit under Major Brocard.
No disease could be an obstacle to a Guynemer when an offensive
was in preparation. In fact, all the Storks were on the spot: Captain
Heurtaux, now recovered from his wound received in Champagne
in April, was in command, and Captain Auger (soon to be killed),
Lieutenant Raymond, Lieutenant Deullin, Lieutenant Lagache
and *sous-lieutenant* Bucquet were there; while Fonck and Verduraz,
newcomers to the squadron but not by any means unknown, Ad-
jutants Guillaumat, Henin, and Petit-Dariel, Sergeants Gaillard and
Moulines, Corporals de Marcy, Dubonnet, and Risacher, completed the staff. As early as June 24 Guynemer had soared again.

In order to realize the importance of this new battle of Flanders which, begun on July 31, was to rage till the following winter, it may not be out of place to quote a German appreciation. In
an issue of the *Lokal Anzeiger*, published at the end of September,
1917, after two months' uninterrupted fighting, Doctor Wegener
wrote as follows:

How can anybody talk of anything but this battle of Flanders? Is it possible that some people actually grow hot over
the parliamentarization, or the loan, or the cost of butter,

or the rumours of peace, while every heart and every eye ought to be fixed on these places where soldiers are doing wonderful deeds! This battle is the most formidable that has yet been fought. It was supposed to be ended, but here it is, blazing afresh and promising a tremendous conflagration. The Englishman goes on with his usual doggedness, and the last bombardment has excelled in horrible intensity all that has been known so far. Even before the signal for storming, the English were drunk with victory, so gigantic was their artillery, so dreadful their guns, so intense their firing....

These lines help us to realize how keen was the anxiety caused in Germany by the new offensive coming so soon after the battles of Champagne in April. But the lyricism of Dr. Wegener stood in the way of his own judgment, and prevented him from seeing that the battle on the Marne which drove the enemy back, the battle on the Yser which brought him to a standstill, and the battle round Verdun which effectually wore him out, were each in succession the greatest of the war. The second battle of Flanders ought rather to be compared to the battle on the Somme, the real consequences of which were not completely visible till the German recoil on the Siegfried line took place in March, 1917. While the first battle of Flanders had closed the gates of Dunkirk and Calais against the Germans, and marked the end of their invasion, the second one drove a wedge at Ypres into the German strength, made formidable by three years' daily efforts, secured the Flemish heights, pushed the enemy back into the bog land, and threatened Bruges. In the first battle, the French under Foch had been supported by the English under Marshal French; this time the English, who were the protagonists, under Plumer (Second Army) and Gough (Fifth Army), were supported by the First French Army under General Anthoine.

It was as late as June that General Anthoine's soldiers had taken their stand to the left of the British armies, and after the tremendous fights along the Chemin des Dames and Moronvillers in April, it might well be believed that they were tired. They had borne the burden from the very first; they had been on the Marne and the Yser in 1914, at the numberless and costly offensives of 1915 in Artois, Champagne, Lorraine and Alsace; and in 1916, after the Verdun epic, they had had to fight on the Somme. Indeed, they had only ceased repelling the enemy's attacks in order to attack in their turn. Among the Allies, they represented invincible determination, as well as a perfected military method. Those troops arriving on June 15, on ground they had never seen before, might well have been anxious for a respite; yet on July 31 they were in the fighting line with the British. Two days before the attack they crossed the Yser canal by twenty-nine bridges without losing one man, and showed an intelligence and spirit which added to their ascendancy over the enemy and increased the prestige of the French army. And while Marshal Haig was finding such an exceptional second in General Anthoine, Pétain, now commander-in-chief, was aiding the British offensive by attacking the Germans at other points on the front: on August 20 the Second Army under Guillaumat was victorious on the Meuse, near Verdun, while the Sixth Army under Maistre was preparing for the Malmaison offensive which on October 23 secured for the French the whole length of the Chemin des Dames to the river Ailette.

General Anthoine had had less than six weeks in which to see what he could do with the ground, organize the lines of communication, and post his batteries and infantry. But he had no idea of delaying the British offensive, and on the appointed day he was ready. The line of attack for the three armies was some 20 kilometres long, namely, from the Ypres-Menin road to the confluence of the Yperlée and Martje-Vaert, the French holding the section between Drie Grachten and Boesinghe. It had been settled that the offensive should be conducted methodically, that its objective should be limited, and that it might be interrupted and resumed as often as should seem advisable. The troops were engaged on the 31st of July, and the first rush carried the French onward a distance of 3 kilometres, not only to Steenstraete, which was the objective, but further on to Bixchoote and the Korteker Tavern. The British on their side had advanced 1500 yards over heavily fortified or wooded ground, and their new line lay along Pilkem, Saint-Julien, Frezenberg, Hooge, Sanctuary Wood, Hollebeke and Basse-Ville. Stormy weather on the first of August, and German counter-attacks on Saint-Julien, prevented an immediate continuation of the offensive, but on August 16 a fresh advance took the French as far as Saint-Jansbeck, while they seized the bridge-head of Drie Grachten. General Anthoine had been so careful in his artillery preparation that one of the attacking battalions had not a single casualty, and no soldier was even wounded. The French then had to wait until the English had advanced in their turn to the range of hillocks between Becelaere and Poelcapelle (September 20 and 26), but the brilliant British successes on those two dates were making another collective operation possible; and this operation took place on October 9, and gave the French possession of the outskirts of Houthulst forest, while the British fought on till they captured the Passchendaele hills.

Every great battle is now preceded and accompanied by a battle in the air, because if chasing or bombarding squadrons did not police the air before an attack, no photographs of the enemy's lines could be taken; and if they did not afford protection for the observers while the troops are engaged, the batteries would shoot and the infantry progress blindly. It is not surprising, therefore, that the enemy, who could not be deceived as to the importance of the French and British preparations in Flanders, had as early as mid-June brought additional aeroplanes and "sausages," and throughout July terrible contests took place in the air. Sometimes these engagements were duels, oftener they were fought by strong squadrons, and on July 13 units consisting of as many as thirty machines were seen on either side, the Germans losing fifteen aeroplanes, and sixteen more going home in a more or less damaged condition.

While in hospital, Guynemer had heard of these tremendous encounters, and wondered if the enchanting cruises he used to make by himself or with just one companion must be things of the past. Was he to be involved in the new tactics and to become a mere unit in a group, or a chief with the responsibility of collective manoeuvres? The air knight was incredulous; he thought of his magic aeroplane and could not persuade himself that, whatever the number of his opponents, he could not single one out for his thunder-clap attack.

****

Meanwhile the artillery preparation had begun, towards the fifteenth of July, and the earth was quaking to the thundering front at a distance of 50 kilometres. These are flat regions, and there would be no beauty in them if the light radiating from the vapours rising from the fields or the sea did not lend brilliance and relief to the yellow stone villages, the straggling woods or copses, the well-to-do farms, the low hedges, or the tall calvaries at the crossroads.

Guynemer was in splendid condition. His indisposition of the previous month had been caused by his refusing to sleep at Dunkirk, as the others did, until their new quarters were ready. He wanted to be near his machine the moment there was light enough to see by, and slept in some unfinished hangar or under canvas in order not to miss any enterprising German who might take advantage of the dusk to sneak over the lines, spy on our preparations, or bombard our rear. He had paid for his imprudence by a severe cold. But now, comfortable-looking wooden houses stood along the shore, and Guynemer was himself again.

On July 27, while patrolling with Lieutenant Deullin, his chum of Somme and of Aisne days—in fact, his friend of much older times—he brought down in flames, between Langemarck and Roulers, a very powerful Albatros, apparently a 220 H.P. of the latest model. This fell far within the enemy lines, but enthusiastic British soldiers witnessed the scene. Guynemer had chosen this Albatros for his victim among eight other machines, and had pulverized it at a distance of a few yards.

This victory was his forty-ninth. He secured his fiftieth the very next day, bringing down a D.F.W. in flames over Westrobeke, the enemy showing fight, for Guynemer's magic aeroplane was hit in the tail, in one of the longitudinal spars, the exhaust pipe, and the hood, and had to be repaired. This day of glory was also one of mourning for the Storks. Captain Auger who, trusting his star after seven triumphs, had gone scouting alone, was shot in the head, and, after mustering energy enough to bring his machine back to the landing-ground, died almost immediately.

Fifty machines destroyed! This had been Guynemer's dream. The apparently inaccessible figure had gradually seemed a possibility. Finally it had become a fact. Fifty machines down, without taking into account those which fell too far from the official observers, or those which had been only disabled, or those which had brought home sometimes a pilot, sometimes a passenger, dead in their seats. What would Guynemer do now? Was he not tired of hunting, killing, or destroying in the high regions of the atmosphere? Did he not feel the exhaustion consequent on the nervous strain of unlimited effort? Could he be entirely deaf to voices which advised him to rest, now that he was a captain, an officer in the Legion of Honour, and, at barely twenty-two, could hardly hope for more distinction? On the other hand, he had shown in his unceasing effort towards an absolutely perfect machine a genius for mechanics which might profitably be given play elsewhere. The occasion was not far to seek, for he had to take his damaged aeroplane back to the works; and what with this interruption and the precarious state of his health—for he had left the hospital too soon—he might reasonably have applied for leave. Nor was this all. The adoption of the new tactics of fighting in numbers might change the nature of his action: he might become the commanding officer of a unit, run less risk, indulge his temerity only once in a while, and yet make himself useful by infusing his own spirit into aspiring pilots.

Slowly all these ideas occurred, if not to him, at all events to his friends. Guynemer has slain his fifty—they must have thought—Guynemer can now rest. What would it matter if some envious people should make remarks?

"It is a pleasure worthy of a king," Alexander once said after Antisthenes, "to hear evil spoken of one while one is doing good."

But Guynemer never knew this royal enjoyment; he never even suspected that well-wishers were plotting for his safety. He took his machine to the works, supervised the repairs with his customary attention, and by August 15 he was back again at his sport in Flanders.

* * * * * * * *

Meanwhile his comrades had added to their laurels. Auger was dead, it is true; but Captain Derode, Adjutant Fonck—a perfect Aymerillot, the smallest and youngest of these knights-errant, Heurtaux, Deullin (both wounded, and the latter now risen to a captaincy), Lieutenant Gorgeus and Corporal Collins—all had done well. Besides them many, too many, bombarding aviators ought to be mentioned, but we must limit ourselves to those who are now laid low in Flemish graveyards: Lieutenant Mulard, Sergeant Thabaud-Deshoulières, *sous-lieutenant* Bailliotz, *sous-lieutenant* Pelletier, who saved his aeroplane if he could not save his own life, and was heard saying to himself before expiring: "For France—I am happy...." finally Lieutenant Ravarra, and Sergeant Delaunay, who had specialized in night attacks and disappeared without ever being heard of again.

Guynemer had reported at the camp on August 15. On the seventeenth, at 9.20 o'clock, he brought down a two-seated Albatros which fell in flames at Wladsloo, and five minutes later a D.F.W. which collapsed, also in flames, south of Dixmude. This double execution avenged the death of Captain Auger and of another Stork, Sergeant Cornet, killed the day before. On the eighteenth, Guynemer poured a broadside, at close quarters, into a two-seated machine above Staden; and on the twentieth, flying this time on his old *Vieux-Charles*, he destroyed a D.F.W. in a quick fight above Poperinghe. This meant three undoubted victories in four days under circumstances which the number of enemy machines and the high altitude made more difficult than they had ever been. The weather during this month of August was constantly stormy, and the Germans were taking every precaution to avoid surprise; but Guynemer was quick as lightning, took advantage of the shortest lulls, and baffled German prudence.

The British or Belgian airmen of the neighbourhood called on him, and he liked to return their politeness. He loved to talk about his methods, especially his shooting methods, for flying to him was only the means of shooting, and once he defined his aeroplane as a flying machine-gun. Captain Galliot, a specialist in gunsmithery, who overheard this remark, also heard him say to the Minister of Aviation, M. Daniel Vincent, who was inspecting the camp at Buc: "It is not by clever flying that you get rid of a Boche, but by hard and sharp shooting."

It is not surprising, therefore, that he began his day's work by overhauling his machine-gun, cartridges, and visor. He did not mind trusting his mechanicians where his aeroplane and motor were concerned, but his weapon and ammunition were his own special care. He regarded as an axiom the well-known maxim of big-game hunters, that "it is not enough to hit, but you must shoot down your enemy with lightning rapidity if you do not wish to perish with him...."[26]

26: *Guynemer tireur de combat* (*Guerre aérienne* for October 18, 1917, special number consecrated to Guynemer).

Of his machine itself Guynemer made a terrible weapon, and he soon passed his fiftieth victory. On August 20 his record numbered fifty-three, and he was in as good condition as on the Somme. On the 24th he was on his way to Paris, planning not only to have his aeroplane repaired, but to point out to the Buc engineers an improvement he had just devised.

CHAPTER 2

Omens

"Oh, yes, the dog always manages to get what he wants," Guynemer's father had once said to him with a sad smile, when Georges, regardless of his two previous failures, insisted at Biarritz upon enlisting.

"The dog? What dog?" Guynemer had answered, not seeing an apologue in his father's words.

"The dog waiting at the door till somebody lets him in. His one thought is to get in while the people's minds are not concentrated on keeping him out. So he is sure to succeed in the end."

It is the same thing with our destiny, waiting till we open the door of our life. Vainly do we try to keep the door tightly shut against it: we cannot think of it all the time, and every now and then we fall into trustfulness, and thus its hour inevitably comes, and from the opening door it beckons to us. M. Bergson says:

What we call fatalism is only the revenge of nature on man's will when the mind puts too much strain upon the flesh or acts as if it did not exist. Orpheus, it is true, charmed the rivers, trees and rocks away from their places with his lyre, but the Maenades tore him to pieces in his turn.

We cannot say that the Guynemer who flew in Flanders was not the same Guynemer who had flown over the Somme, Lorraine or Aisne battlefields. Indeed, his mastery was increasing with each fresh encounter, and with his daring he cared little whether the enemy was gaining in numbers or inventing unsuspected tactics. His victories of August 17 and 20 showed him at his boldest best. Yet his comrades noticed that his nerves seemed overstrained. He was not content with flying oftener and longer than the others in quest of his game, but fretted if his Boche did not appear precisely when he wanted him. When an enemy did not turn up where he was expected, he made up his mind to seek him where he himself was not expected, and he became accustomed to scouting farther and farther away into dangerous zones. Was he tired of holding the door tight against destiny, or feeling sure that destiny could not look in? Did it not occur to him that his hour, whether near or not, was marked down?

Indeed, it is certain that the thought not only presented itself to him sometimes, but was familiar. Lieutenant Constantin his school-fellow of Stanislas days writes:

At our last meeting I had been struck by his melancholy expression, and yet he had just been victorious for the forty-seventh time. 'I have been too lucky,' he said to me, 'and I feel as if I must pay for it.' 'Nonsense,' I replied, 'I am absolutely certain that nothing will happen to you.' He smiled as if he did not believe me, but I knew that he was haunted by the idea, and avoided everything that might uselessly consume a particle of his energy or disturb his sang-froid, which he intended to devote entirely to Boche hunting.[27]

When had he ceased to think himself invincible? The reader no doubt remembers how he recovered from his wound at Verdun, and the shock it might have left, merely by flying and offering himself to the enemy's fire with the firm resolve not to return it. Eight times he had been brought down, and each time with full and prolonged consciousness of what was happening. On many occasions he had come back to camp with bullets in his machine, or in his combination. Yet these narrow escapes never reacted on his imagination, damped his spirit, or diminished his *furia*. But had he thought himself invincible? He believed in his star, no doubt, but he knew he was only a man. One of his most intimate friends, his rival in glory, the nearest to him since the loss of Dormé, the one who was the Oliver to this Roland, once received this confidence from Guynemer: "One of the fellows told me that when he starts up he only thinks of the fighting before him; he found that sufficiently absorbing; but I told him that

27: Unpublished notes by J. Constantin.

162

when the men start my motor I always make a sign to the fellows standing around. 'Yes, I have seen it,' he answered; 'the handshake of the airman. It means *au revoir.*' But maybe it is farewell I am inwardly saying," Guynemer added, and laughed, for the boy in him was never far from the man.

* * * * * * * *

Towards the end of July, while he was in Paris seeing to the repairs for his machine after bringing down his fiftieth enemy, he had gone to Compiègne for a short visit. His father, knowing his technical ability and his interest in all mechanical improvements, and on the other hand noticing a nervousness in his manner, dared for the first time to hint timidly and allusively at the possibility of his being useful in some other field.

"Couldn't you be of service with respect to making engines, etc?"

But he was embarrassed by his son's look of questioning surprise. Every time Guynemer had used his father's influence in the army, it had been to bring himself nearer to danger.

"No man has the right to get away from the front as long as the war lasts," he said. "I see very well what you are thinking, but you know that self-sacrifice is never wasted. Don't let us talk any more about it...."

On Tuesday, August 28, Guynemer, having been obliged to come to Paris again for repairs to his aeroplane, went to Saint-Pierre de Chaillot. It was not exceptional for him to visit this old church; he loved to prepare himself there for his battle. One of the officiating priests has written since his death of "his faith and the transparency of his soul."[28] The Chaillot parishioners knew him well, but pretended not to notice him, and he thought himself one in a crowd. After seeing the priest in the confessional, he usually enjoyed another little chat in the sacristy, and although he was no man for long prayers and meditations, he expressed his thoughts on such occasions in heartfelt and serious language.

"My fate is sealed," he once said in his playful, authoritative way; "I cannot escape it." And remembering his not very far away Latin, he added: "*Hodie mihi, cras tibi....*"

* * * * * * * *

Early in September he made up his mind to go back to Flan-

28: *La Croix*, October 7, 1917, article by Pierre l'Ermite.

ders, although his aeroplane was not yet entirely repaired. The day before leaving he was standing at the door of the Hôtel Edouard VII when one of his schoolmates at the Collège Stanislas, Lieutenant Jacquemin, appeared, this officer relates:

> He took me to his room and we talked for more than an hour about schooldays. I asked him whether he had some special dodge to be so successful. 'None whatever,' he said, 'but you remember I took a prize for shooting at Stanislas. I shoot straight, and have absolute confidence in my machine.' He showed me his numberless decorations, and was just as simple and full of good fellowship as he was at Stanislas. It was evident that his head had not been in the least turned by his success; he only talked more and enjoyed describing his fights. He told me, too, that in spite of opposition from aeroplane builders he had secured a long-contemplated improvement; and that he had had a special camera made for him with which he could photograph a machine as it fell. His parting words were: 'I hope to fly tomorrow, but don't expect to see my name any more in the communiqués. That's all over: I have bagged my fifty Boches.'

Were not these strange words, if indeed Guynemer attached any meaning to them? At all events, they expressed his innermost longing, which was to go on flying, even if he should fly for nothing.

* * * * * * * *

Before reporting at Dunkirk, Guynemer spent September 2, 3, and 4 with his people at Compiègne. Never was he more fascinatingly affectionate, boyish, and bright than during those three days. But he seemed agitated. "Let us make plans," he said repeatedly, in spite of his old aversion to castle-building. His plans that day were for the amusement of his sisters. He reminded the younger, Yvonne, that he had quarrelled once with her. It was at Biarritz, when he wanted her to make a *novena* (nine days' special prayers) that he might not be rejected by the recruiting board again; his sister did not like to promise, and he had threatened to sulk forever, which he had proceeded to do—for five minutes.

His mother and sisters thought him more enchanting than ever, but his father felt that he was overstrained, and realized that his almost morbid notion of his duty as a chaser who could no longer wait for his chance but wanted to force a victory, was the result of fatigue. M. Guynemer no longer hesitated to speak, adding that the period of rest he advised was in the very interest of his son's service. "You need strengthening; you have done too much. If you should go on, you would be in great danger of falling below yourself, or not really being yourself."

"Father, war is nothing else. One must pull on, even if the rope should threaten to snap."

It was the first time that M. Guynemer had given undisguised advice, and he urged his point.

"Why not stop awhile? Your record is pretty good; you might form younger pilots, and in time go back to your squadron."

"Yes, and people would say that, hoping for no more distinctions, I have given up fighting."

"What does it matter? Let people talk, and when you reappear in better condition they will understand. You know I never gave you a word of advice which the whole world could not hear. I always helped you, and you always found the most disinterested approval here in your home. But you will admit that human strength has its limits."

"Yes," Georges interposed, "a limit which we must endeavour to leave behind. We have given nothing as long as we have not given everything."

M. Guynemer said no more. He felt that he had probed his son's soul to the depths, and his pride in his hero did not diminish his sorrow. When they parted he concealed his anguish, but he watched the boy, thinking he would never see him again. His wife and daughters, too, stood on the threshold oppressed by the same feelings, trying to suppress their anxiety and finding no words to veil it.

In the Iliad, Hector, after breaking into the Greek camp like a dark whirlwind unexpectedly sweeping the land, and which the gods alone could stop, returns to Troy and stopping at the Scaean gates waits for Achilles, who he knows must be wild to avenge Patroclus. Old Priam sees his son's danger, and beseeches him not to seek his antagonist. Hecuba joins her tears to his supplications. But tears and entreaties avail little, and Hector, turning a deaf ear to his parents, walks out to meet Achilles, as he thinks, but indeed to meet his own fate.

On September 4, Guynemer was at the flying field of Saint-Pol-sur-Mer near Dunkirk. His old friend, Captain Heurtaux, so long Commander of the Storks, was not there; he had been wounded the day before by an explosive bullet, and the English had picked up and evacuated him. Heurtaux possessed infinite tact, and had not infrequently succeeded in influencing the rebellious Guynemer; but nobody was there to replace him. September 5 was a day of extraordinary activity for Guynemer. His magic aeroplane was still at the works, where he had complained of not having another in reserve; and not being able to wait for it, he sent for his old machine and immediately attacked a D.F.W. at close quarters, as usual; but the Boche was saved by the jamming of both of Guynemer's guns, and the aviator had to get back to his landing-ground. Furious at this failure, he promptly soared up again and attacked a chain of five one-seated planes, hitting two, which however managed to protect each other and escape. After two hours and a half, Guynemer went home again, overhauled his guns, found a trigger out of order, and for the third time went up again, scouring the sky for two more hours, indignant to see nothing but prudent Germans keeping far out of his reach. So, he had flown five hours and a half in that one day. What nerves could stand such a strain? But Guynemer, seeking victory, cared little for strain or nerves. Everything seemed to go against him: Heurtaux away, his best machine not available, his machine-guns out of order, and Germans refusing his challenge. No wonder if he fretted himself into increased irritation.

* * * * * * * *

Guynemer liked Lieutenant Raymond, and every now and then flew with him. This officer being on leave, Guynemer on September 8 asked another favourite comrade, sous-lieutenant Bozon-Verduraz, to accompany him. The day was sullen, and a thick fog soon parted the two aviators, who lost their way and only managed to get clear of the fog when Bozon-Verduraz was over Nieuport and Guynemer over Ostend.

September 9 was a Sunday, and Guynemer over-slept and had to be roused by a friend.

"Aren't you coming to mass?"

"Of course."

GOING WEST

The two officers went to mass at Saint-Pol-sur-Mer, and the weather having grown worse Guynemer did not fly; but instead of enjoying the enforced rest, he resented it as a personal wrong. Next day he flew three times, and was unlucky again every time. On his first flight, on his two-gun machine, he found that the water-pump control did not work, and had to land on a Belgian aerodrome, where he was welcomed and asked to sit for his photograph. The picture shows a worried, tense, disquieting countenance under the mask ready to be pulled down. After frightening the enemy so long, Guynemer was now frightening his friends.

The photograph taken, Guynemer flew back to camp. The best for him, under the circumstances, would have been to wait. Was he not hourly to hear that he might go to the Buc works for his machine? And what was the use of flying on an unsatisfactory aeroplane? But Guynemer was not in Flanders to wait. He wanted his quarry, and he wanted to set an example to and galvanize his men, and even the infantry. So, Deullin being absent, Guynemer borrowed his machine, and at last discovered a chain of German flyers, whom he attacked regardless of their number. But four bullets hit his machine and one damaged the air-pump, an accident which not only compelled him to land but to return by motor to the aerodrome. Once more, instead of listening to the whisper of wisdom, he started, on Lieutenant Lagache's machine; and this time the annoyance was the gasoline spurting over the loose top of the carburettor. The oil caught fire, and Guynemer had to give in, having failed three times, and having been in the air five hours and a half on unsatisfactory aeroplanes. No wonder if, with the weather, the machines, and circumstances generally against him, he felt tired and nervous. He had never done so much with such poor results. But his will, his will cannot accept what is forced upon him, and we may be sure that he will not acknowledge himself beaten.

CHAPTER 3

The Last Flight

On Tuesday, September 11, the weather was once more uncertain. But morning fogs by the seaside do not last, and the sun soon began to shine. Guynemer had had a restless night after his failures, and had brooded, as irritable people do, over the very things that made him fretful. Chasing without his new aeroplane—the enchanting machine which he had borne in his mind so many months, as a women bears her child, and which at last he had felt soaring under him—was no pleasure. He missed it so much that the feeling became an obsession, until he made up his mind to leave for Buc before the day was over. Indeed, he would have done so sooner had he not been haunted by the idea that he must first bring down his Boche. But since the Boche did not seem to be willing.... Now he is resolved, and more calm; he will go to Paris this very evening. He has only to while away the time till the train is due. The prospect in itself is quieting, and besides Major du Peuty, one of the chiefs of Aviation at headquarters, and Major Brocard, recently appointed attaché to the Minister of Aeronautics, were coming down by the early train. They were sure to arrive at the camp between nine and ten, and a conversation with them could not but be instructive and illuminating; so, better wait for them.

But, in spite of these tranquillizing thoughts, Guynemer was restless, and his face showed the sallow colour which always foreboded his physical relapses. His mind was not really made up, and he would come and go, strolling from his tent to the sheds and from the sheds to his tent. He was not cross, only nervous. Suddenly he went back to the shed and examined his *Vieux-Charles*. Why, the machine was not so bad after all; the motor and guns had been repaired, and yesterday's accident was not likely to happen again. If so, why not fly? In the absence of Heurtaux, Guynemer was in command, and once more the necessity of setting a good example forced itself upon him. Several flyers had started on scouting work already; the fog was quickly lifting, the day would soon be resplendent, and the notion of duty too quickly dazzled him, like the sun. For duty had always been his motive power; he had always anticipated it, from the day when he was fighting to enlist at Biarritz to this 11th of September, 1917. It was neither the passion for glory nor the craze to be an aviator which had caused him to join, but his longing to be of use; and in the same way his last flights were made in obedience to his will to serve.

All at once he was really resolved. *sous-lieutenant* Bozon-Verduraz was requested to accompany him, and the mechanicians wheeled the machines out. One of his comrades asked with assumed negligence: "Aren't you going to wait till Major du Peuty and Major Brocard arrive?"

Guynemer's only answer was to wave towards the sky then freeing itself from its veils of fog as he himself was shaking off his hesitancy, and his friend felt that he must not be urgent. Everybody of late had noticed his nervousness, and Guynemer knew it and resented it; tact was more necessary than ever with him. Let it be remembered that he was the pet, almost the spoiled child, of his service, and that it had never been easy to approach him. Meanwhile, the two majors, who had been met at the station, were told of his nervous condition, and hurried to speak to him. They expected to reach the camp by nine o'clock, and would send for him at once. But Guynemer and Bozon-Verduraz had started at twenty-five minutes past eight.

They had left the sea behind them, flying south-east. They had reached the lines, following them over Bixchoote and the Korteker Tavern which the French troops had taken on July 31, over the Bixchoote-Langemarck road, and finally over Langemarck itself, captured by the British on August 16. Trenches, sections of broken roads, familiar to them from above, crossed and recrossed each other under them, and they descried to the north of Langemarck road the railway, or what used to be the railway, between Ypres and Thourout and the Saint-Julien-Poelkapelle road. No German patrol appeared above the French or British lines, which Guynemer and his companion lost sight of above the Maison Blanche, and they followed on to the German lines over the faint vestiges of Poelkapelle.

Guynemer's keen, long-practiced eye then saw a two-seated enemy aeroplane flying alone lower down than himself, and a signal was made to attract Bozon-Verduraz' notice. A fight was certain, and this fight was the one which Fate had long decided on. The attack on a two-seater flying over its own lines, and consequently enjoying unrestricted freedom of movement, is known to be a ticklish affair, as the pilot can shoot through the propeller and the passenger in his turret rakes the whole field of vision with the exception of two angles, one in front, the other behind him under the fuselage and tail. Facing the enemy and shooting directly at him, whether upwards or downwards, was Guynemer's method; but it is not easy on account of the varying speeds of the two machines, and because the pilot as well as the passenger is sheltered by the engine. So it is best to get behind and a little lower than the tail of the enemy plane.

Guynemer had frequently used this manoeuvre, but he preferred a front attack, thinking that if he should fail he could easily resort to the other, either by turning or by a quick tail spin. So he tried to get between the sun and the enemy; but as ill-luck would have it, the sky clouded over, and Guynemer had to dive down to his opponent's level, so as to show him only the thin edges of the planes, hardly visible. But by this time the German had noticed him, and was endeavouring to get his range. Prudence advised *zigzagging*, for a cool-headed gunner has every chance of hitting a straight-flying aeroplane; the enemy ought to be made to shift his aim by quick tacking, and the attack should be made from above with a full volley, with the possibility of dodging back in case the enemy is not brought down at once. But Guynemer, regardless of rules and stratagems, merely fell on his enemy like a cannon ball. He might have said, like Alexander refusing to take advantage of the dark against Darius, that he did not want to steal victory. He only counted on his lightning-like manner of charging, which had won him so many victories, and on his marksmanship. But he missed the German, who proceeded to tail spin, and was missed again by Bozon-Verduraz, who awaited him below.

What ought Guynemer to do? Desist, no doubt. But, having been imprudent in his direct attack, he was imprudent again on his new tack, and his usual obstinacy, made worse by irritation, counselled him to a dangerous course. As he dived lower and lower in hopes of being able to wheel around and have another shot, Bozon-Verduraz spied a chain of eight German one-seaters above the British lines. It was agreed between him and his chief that on such occasions he should offer himself to the newcomers, allure, entice, and throw them off the track, giving Guynemer time to achieve his fifty-fourth success, after which he should fly round again to where the fight was going on. He had no anxiety about Guynemer, with whom he had frequently attacked enemy squadrons of five, six, or even ten or twelve one-seaters. The two-seater might, no doubt, be more dangerous, and Guynemer had recently seemed nervous and below par; but in a fight his presence of mind, infallibility of movement, and quickness of eye were sure to come back, and the two-seater could hardly escape its doom.

The last image imprinted on the eyes of Bozon-Verduraz was of Guynemer and the German both spinning down, Guynemer in search of a chance to shoot, the other hoping to be helped from down below. Then Bozon-Verduraz had flown in the direction of the eight one-seaters, and the group had fallen apart, chasing him. In time the eight machines became mere specks in the illimitable sky, and Bozon-Verduraz, seeing he had achieved his object, flew back to where his chief was no doubt waiting for him. But there was nobody in the empty space. Could it be that the German had escaped? With deadly anguish oppressing him, the airman descended nearer the ground to get a closer view. Down below there was nothing, no sign, none of the bustle which always follows the falling of an aeroplane. Feeling reassured, he climbed again and began to circle round and round, expecting his comrade. Guynemer was coming back, could not but come back, and the cause of his delay was probably the excitement of the chase. He was so reckless! Like Dormé—who one fine morning in May, on the Aisne, went out and was never heard of afterwards—he was not afraid of travelling long distances over enemy country. He must come back. It is impossible he should not come back; he was beyond the reach of common accidents, invincible, immortal! This was a certitude, the very faith of the Storks, a tenet which never was questioned. The notion of Guynemer falling to a German seemed hardly short of sacrilege.

So Bozon-Verduraz waited on, making up his mind to wait as long as necessary. But an hour passed, and nobody appeared. Then the airman broadened his circles and searched farther out, without, however, swerving from the rallying-point. He searched the air like Nisus the forest in his quest of Euryalus, and his mind began to misgive him.

After two hours he was still waiting, alone, noticing with dismay that his oil was running low. One more circle! How slack the engine sounded to him! One more circle! Now it was impossible to wait any more: he must go back alone.

On landing, his first word was to ask about Guynemer.

"Not back yet!"

Bozon-Verduraz knew it. He knew that Guynemer had been taken away from him. The telephone and the wireless sent their appeals around, aeroplanes started on anxious cruises. Hour followed hour, and evening came, one of those late summer evenings during which the horizon wears the tints of flowers; the shadows deepened, and no news came of Guynemer. From neighbouring camps French, British, or Belgian comrades arrived, anxious for news. Everywhere the latest birds had come home, and one hardly dared ask the airmen any question.

But the daily routine had to be dispatched, as if there were no mourning in the camp. All the young men there were used to death, and to sporting with it; they did not like to show their sorrow; but it was deep in them, sullen and fierce.

At dinner a heavy melancholy weighed upon them. Guynemer's seat was empty, and no one dreamed of taking it. One officer tried to dispel the cloud by suggesting hypotheses. Guynemer was lucky, had always been; probably he was alive, a prisoner. Guynemer a prisoner!... He had said one day with a laugh, "The Boches will never get me alive," but his laugh was terrible. No, Guynemer could not have been taken prisoner. Where was he, then? On the squadron log, *sous-lieutenant* Bozon-Verduraz wrote that evening as follows:

Tuesday, September 11, 1917. Patrolled. Captain Guynemer started at 8.25 with *sous-lieutenant* Bozon-Verduraz. Found missing after an engagement with a biplane above Poelkapelle (Belgium).

That was all.

CHAPTER 4

The Vigil

Before Guynemer, other knights of the air, other aces, had been reported missing or had perished—some like Captain Le Cour Grandmaison or Captain Auger in our lines, others like Sergeant Sauvage and *sous-lieutenant* Dormé in the enemy's. In fact, he would be the thirteenth on the list if the title of ace is reserved for aviators to whom the controlling board has given its *visé* for five undoubted victories. These were the names:

Captain Le Cour Grandmaison	5 victories
Sergeant Hauss	5 victories
Sous-Lieutenant Delorme	5 victories
Sous-Lieutenant Pégoud	6 victories
Sous-Lieutenant Languedoc	7 victories
Captain Auger	7 victories
Captain Doumer	7 victories
Sous-Lieutenant Rochefort	7 victories
Sergeant Sauvage	8 victories
Captain Matton	9 victories
Adjutant Lenoir	11 victories
Sous-Lieutenant Dormé	23 victories

Would Guynemer's friends now have to add: Captain Guynemer, 53? Nobody dared to do so, yet nobody now dared hope.

A poet of genius, who even before the war had been an aviator, Gabriele d'Annunzio, has described in his novel, *Forse che si forse che no*, the friendship of two young men, Paolo Tarsis and Giulio Cambasio, whose mutual affection, arising from a similar longing to conquer the sky, has grown in the perils they dare together. If this book had been written later, war would have intensified its meaning. Instead of dying in a fight, Cambasio is killed in a contest for altitude between Bergamo and the Lake of Garda. As Achilles watched beside the dead body of Patroclus, so Tarsis would not leave to another the guarding of his lost friend:

> In tearless grief Paolo Tarsis kept vigil through the short summer night. So it had broken asunder the richest bough on the tree of his life; the most generous part of himself ruined. For him the beauty of war had diminished, now that he was no longer to see, burning in those dead eyes, the fervour of effort, the security of confidence, the rapidity of resolution. He was no longer to taste the two purest joys of a manly heart: steadiness of eye in attack, and the pride of watching over a beloved peer.

For him the beauty of war had diminished.... War already so long, so exhausting and cruel, and laden with sorrow! Will war appear in its horrid nakedness, now that those who invested it with glory disappear, now, above all, when the king of these heroes, the dazzling young man whose luminous task was known to the whole army, is no more? Is not his loss the loss of something akin to life? For a Guynemer is like the nation's flag: if the soldiers' eyes miss the waving colours, they may wander to the wretchedness of daily routine, and morbidly feed on blood and death. This is what the loss of a Guynemer might mean.

But can a Guynemer be quite lost?

* * * * * * * *

From the author's diary

Saint-Pol-sur-Mer, September, 1917
Visited the Storks Escadrille.
The flying field occupies a vast space, for it is common to the French and the British. A dam protecting the landing-ground screens it from the sea. But from the second floor of a little house which the bombs have left standing, you can see its moving expanse of a delicate, I might say timid blue, dotted with home-coming boats. The evening is placid and fine, with a reddish haze blurring the horizon.

Opposite the sheds, with their swelling canvas walls, a row

of aeroplanes is standing before being rolled in for the night. The mechanicians feel them with careful hands, examining the engines, propellers, and wings. The pilots are standing around, still in their leather suits, their helmets in their hands. In brief sentences they sum up their day's experiences.

Mechanically I look among them for the one whom the eye invariably sought first. I recalled his slight figure, his amber complexion, and dark, wonderful eyes, and his quick descriptive gestures. I remembered his ringing, boyish laugh, as he said:

"And then, *couic*...."

He was life itself. He got out of his seat panting but radiant, quivering, as it were, like the bow-string when it has sent its shaft, and full of the sacred drunkenness of a young god.

Ten days had passed since his disappearance. Nothing more was known than on that eleventh of September when Bozon-Verduraz came back alone. German prisoners belonging to aviation had not heard that he was reported missing. Yet it was inconceivable that such a piece of news should not have been circulated; and, in fact, yesterday a message dropped by a German aeroplane on the British lines, concerning several English aviators killed or in hospital, was completed by a note saying that Captain Guynemer had been brought down at Poelkapelle on September 10, at 8 a.m. But could this message be credited? Both the day and hour it stated were wrong. On September 10 at 8 a.m. Guynemer was alive, and even the next day he had not left the camp at the hour mentioned. An English newspaper had announced his disappearance, and perhaps the enemy was merely using the information. The mystery remained unsolved.

As we were discussing these particulars, the last aeroplanes were landing, one after another, and Guynemer's companions offered their reasons for hoping, or rather believing; but none seemed convinced by his own arguments. Their inner conviction must be that their young chief is dead; and besides, what is death, what is life, to devoting one's all to France?

Captain d'Harcourt had succeeded Major Brocard pro tem as commandant of the unit. He was a very slim, very elegant young man, with the grace and courtesy of the *ancien régime* which his name evoked, and the perfection of his manners and gentleness seemed to lend convincing power to all he said. Guynemer being missing and Heurtaux wounded, the Storks were now commanded by Lieutenant Raymond. He belonged to the cavalry, a tall, thin man, with the sharp face and heroic bearing of Don Quixote, a kindly man with a roughness of manner and a quick, picturesque way of expressing himself. Deullin was there, too, one of Guynemer's oldest and most devoted friends. Last of all descended from the high regions *sous-lieutenant* Bozon-Verduraz, a rather heavy man with a serious face, and more maturity than belonged to his years, an unassuming young man with a hatred for exaggeration and a deep respect for the truth.

Once more he went through every detail of the fatal day for me, each particular anticipating the dread issue. But in spite of this narrative, full of the idea of death, I could not think of Guynemer as dead and lying somewhere under the ground held by the enemy. It was impossible for me not to conjure up Guynemer alive and even full of life, Guynemer chasing the enemy with strained terrible eyes, Guynemer of the superhuman will, the Guynemer who never gave up,— in short, a Guynemer whom death could not vanquish.

A wonderful atmosphere men breathe here, for it relieves death of its horror. One officer, Raymond, I think, said in a careless manner:

"Guynemer's fate will be ours, of course."

Somebody protested: "The country needs men like you."

To which Deullin answered: "Why does it? There will be others after us, and the life we lead...."

But Captain d'Harcourt broke in gaily: "Come on; dinner's ready—and with this bright moon and clear sky we are sure to get bombed."

Bombed, indeed, we were, and pretty severely, but in convenient time, for we had just drunk our coffee. A few minutes before, the practiced ear of one of us had caught the sound of the *bimoulins*, the bi-motor German aeroplanes, and soon they were near. We gained the sheltering trench. But the night was so entrancingly pure, with the moon riding like an airship in the deep space, that it seemed to promise peace and invited us to enjoy the spectacle. We climbed upon the parapet and listened to the breathing of the sea, accompanying with its bass the music of the motors. There were still a few straggling reddish vapours over the luminous landscape, and the stars seemed dim. But other stars took their place, those of the French *Voisins* returning from some bombing expedition, their lights dotting the sky like a moving constellation, while at intervals a rocket shot from one or the other who was anxious not to miss the landing-ground. Over Dunkirk, eight or ten searchlights stretched out their long white arms, thrusting and raking to and fro after the enemy machines. Suddenly one of these appeared, dazzled by the revealing light, as a moth in the circle of a lamp; our batteries began firing, and we could see the quick sparks of their shells all around it. Flashing bullets, too, drew zebra-like stripes across the sky, and with the cannonade and the rumbling of the aeroplanes we heard the lament of the Dunkirk sirens announcing the dreaded arrival of the huge 380 shells upon the town, where here and there fires broke out. Meanwhile the German aeroplanes got rid of their bombs all around us, and we could feel the ground tremble.

The Storks looked on with the indifference of habit, thinking of their beds and awaiting the end. One of them, a weather prophet, said:

"It will be a good day tomorrow; we can start early."

As I spun towards Dunkirk in the motor, these young men and their speeches were in my mind, and I seemed to hear them speaking of their absent companion without any depression, with hardly any sorrow. They thought of him when they were successful, referred to him as a model, found an incentive in his memory,—that was all. Their grief over his loss was virile and invigorating.

* * * * * * * *

After watching his friend's body through the night, the hero of d'Annunzio goes to the aerodrome where the next trials for altitude are to take place. He cannot think of robbing the dead man of his victory. As he rises into the upper regions of the air he feels a soothing influence and an increase of power: the dead man himself pilots his machine, wields the controls, and helps him higher, ever higher up in divine intoxication.

In the same way the warlike power of Guynemer's companions is not diminished. Guynemer is still with them, accompanying each one, and instilling into them the passionate longing to do more and more for France.

CHAPTER 5

The Legend

In seaside graveyards, the stone crosses above the empty tombs say only, after the name, "Lost at sea." I remember also seeing in the churchyards of the Vale of Chamonix similar inscriptions: "Lost on Mont-Blanc." As the mountains and the sea sometimes refuse to give up their victims, so the air seems to have kept Guynemer.

"He was neither seen nor heard as he fell," M. Henri Lavedan wrote at the beginning of October; his body and his machine were never found. Where has he gone? By what wings did he manage thus to glide into immortality? Nobody knows: nothing is known. He ascended and never came back, that is all. Perhaps our descendants will say: "He flew so high that he could not come down again."[29]

I remember a strange line read in some Miscellany in my youth and never forgotten, though the rest of the poem has vanished from memory:

Un jet d'eau qui montait n'est pas redescendu.

Does this not embody the upspringing force of Guynemer's brilliant youth?

Throughout France some sort of miracle was expected: Guynemer must reappear—if a prisoner he must escape, if dead he must come to life. His father said he would go on believing even to the extreme limits of improbability. The journalist who signs his letters from the front to *Le Temps* with the pseudonym d'Entraygues recalled a passage from Balzac in which some peasants at work on a haystack call to the postman on the road:

29: *L'Illustration*, October 6, 1917.

"What's the news?"

"Nothing, no news. Oh! I beg your pardon, people say that Napoleon has died at St. Helena."

Work stops at once, and the peasants look at one another in silence. But one fellow standing on the rick says:

"Napoleon dead! *psha!* it's plain those people don't know him!"

The journalist added that he heard a speech of the same kind in the bush-region of Aveyron. A passenger on the motor-bus read in a newspaper the news of Guynemer's death; everybody seemed dismayed. The chauffeur alone smiled sceptically as he examined the spark plugs of his engine. When he had done, he pulled down the hood, put away his spectacles, carefully wiped his dirty hands on a cloth still dirtier, and planting himself in front of the passenger said:

"Very well. I tell you that the man who is to down Guynemer is still an apprentice. Do you understand?..."

The credulity of the poor people of France with regard to their hero was most touching. When the death of Guynemer had to be admitted, there was deep mourning, from Paris to the remote villages where news travels slowly, but is long pondered upon. Guynemer had been brought down from a height of 700 metres, northeast of Poelkapelle cemetery, in the Ypres sector. A German non-commissioned officer and two soldiers had immediately gone to where the machine was lying. One of the wings of the machine was broken; the airman had been shot through the head, and his leg and shoulder had been broken in the fall; but his face was untouched, and he had been identified at once by the photograph on his pilot's diploma. A military funeral had been given to him.

Nevertheless, it seemed as if Guynemer's fate still remained somewhat obscure. The German War Office published a list of French machines fallen in the German lines, with the official indications by which they had been recognized. Now, the number of the *Vieux-Charles* did not appear on any of these lists, although having only one wing broken the number ought to have been plainly visible. Who were the non-commissioned officer and the two soldiers? Finally, on October 4, 1917, the British took Poelkapelle, but the enemy counter-attacked, and there was furious fighting. On the 9th the village was completely occupied by the British, and they searched for Guynemer's grave. No trace of it could be found in either the military or the village graveyard.

In fact, the Germans had to acknowledge in an official document that both the body and the aeroplane of Guynemer had disappeared. On November 8, 1917, the German Foreign Office replied as follows to a question asked by the Spanish Ambassador:

Captain Guynemer fell in the course of an air fight on September 11 at ten a.m. close to the honour graveyard No. 2 south of Poelkapelle. A surgeon found that he had been shot through the head, and that the forefinger of his left hand had been shot off by a bullet. The body could neither be buried nor removed, as the place had been since the previous day under constant and heavy fire, and during the following days it was impossible to approach it. The sector authorities communicate that the shelling had ploughed up the entire district, and that no trace could be found on September 12 of either the body or the machine. Fresh inquiries, which were made in order to answer the question of the Spanish Embassy, were also fruitless, as the place where Captain Guynemer fell is now in the possession of the British.

The German airmen express their regret at having been unable to render the last honours to a valiant enemy.

It should be added that investigation in this case was only made with the greatest difficulty, as the enemy was constantly attacking, fresh troops were frequently brought in or relieved, and eye witnesses had either been killed or wounded, or transferred. Our troops being continually engaged have not been in a position to give the aforesaid information sooner.

So there had been no military funeral, and Guynemer had accepted nothing from his enemies, not even a wooden cross. The battle he had so often fought in the air had continued around his body; the Allied guns had kept the Germans away from it. So nobody can say where lies what was left of Guynemer: and no hand had touched him. Dead though he was, he escaped. He who was life and movement itself, could not accept the immobility of the tomb.

German applause, like that with which the Greeks welcomed the dead body of Hector, did not fail to welcome Guynemer's end. At the end of three weeks a coarse and discourteous paean was sung in the *Woche*. In its issue of October 6, this paper devoted to Guynemer, under the title "Most Successful French Aviator Killed," an article whose lying cowardice is enough to disgrace a newspaper, and which ought to be preserved to shame it. A reproduction of Guynemer's diploma was given with the article, which ran as follows:

> Captain Guynemer enjoyed high reputation in the French army, as he professed having brought down more than fifty aeroplanes, but many of these were proved to have got back to their camps, though damaged it is true. The French, in order to make all verification on our side impossible, have given up stating, in the past few months, the place or date of their so-called victories. Certain French aviators, taken prisoner by our troops, have described his method thus: sometimes, when in command of his squadron, he left it to his men to attack, and when he had ascertained which of his opponents was the weakest, he attacked that one in turn. Sometimes he would fly alone at very great altitudes, for hours, above his own lines, and when he saw one of our machines separated from the others would pounce upon it unawares. If his first onset failed, he would desist at once, not liking fights of long duration, in the course of which real gallantry must be displayed.[30]

This is the filth the German paper was not ashamed to print. Repulsive though it is, I must analyze some of its details. An enemy's abuse reveals his own character. So this German denied the fifty-three victories of Guynemer, all controlled, and with such severity that in his case, as in that of Dormé, he was not credited with

30: *Der Erfolgreichste Französische Kampfflieger Gefallen. Kapitän Guynemer genoss grossen Ruhm im französischen Heere, da er 50 Flugzeuge abgeschossen haben wollte. Von diesen ist jedoch nachgewiesenermassen eine grosse Zahl, wenn auch beschädigt, in ihre Flughäfen zurückgekert. Um deutscherseits eine Nachprüfung unmöglich zu machen, wurden in den letzten Monaten Ort und Datum seiner angeblichen Luftsiege nicht mehr angegeben. Ueber seine Kampfmethode haben gefangene französische Flieger berichtet: Entweder liess er, als Geschwaderführer fliegend, seine Kameraden zuerst angreifen un stürzle sich dann erst auf den schwächsten Gegner; oder er flog stundenlang in grössten Höhe, allein hinter der französischen Front und stürzte sich von oben herab überraschend auf einzeln fliegende deutsche Beobachtungsflugzeuge. Hatte Guynemer beim ersten Verstoss keinen Erfolg, so brach er das Gefecht sofort ab; auf den länger dauernden, wahrhaft muterprobenden Kurvenkampf liess er sich nicht gern ein.*—Extract from the *Woche* of October 6, 1917.

fully a third of his distant triumphs, too far away to be officially recognized; so this German also vilified Guynemer's fighting methods, Guynemer the foolhardy, the wildly, madly foolhardy, whose machines and clothes were everlastingly riddled with bullets, who fought at such close quarters that he was constantly in danger of collisions—this Guynemer the German journalist makes out to be a prudent and timid airman, shirking fight and making use of his comrades. What sort of story had the German who brought him down told? Was it not obvious that if Guynemer had engaged him at 4000 metres, and had been killed at 700, that he must have prolonged the struggle, and prolonged it above the enemy's lines? Finally, the German journalist had the unutterable meanness and infamy to saddle on imprisoned French aviators this slander of their comrade, insinuated rather than boldly expressed. After all, this document is invaluable, and ought to be framed and preserved. How Guynemer would have laughed over it, and how youthfully ringing and honest the laugh would have sounded! Villiers de l'Isle Adam, remembering the Hegelian philosophy, once wrote:

> The man who insults you only insults the idea he has formed of you, that is to say, himself.

As a whole army (the Sixth) marched on May 25 towards that hill of the Aisne valley where Guynemer had brought down four German machines, and acclaimed his triumph, so the whole French nation would take part in mourning him.

At the funeral service held at Saint Antony's Compiègne, the Bishop of Beauvais, Monseigneur Le Senne, spoke, taking for his text the Psalm in which David laments the death of Saul and his sons slain *on the summits*, and says that this calamity must be kept secret lest the Philistines and their daughters should rejoice over it. This service was attended by General Débeney, staff major-general, representing the *generalissimo*, and by all the surviving members of the Storks Escadrille, with their former chief, Major Brocard. His successor, Captain Heurtaux, whose unexpected appearance startled the congregation—he seemed so pale and thin on his crutches—had left the hospital for this ceremony, and looked so ill that people were surprised that he had the strength to stand.

A few hours before the service took place, Major Garibaldi, sent by General Anthoine, commander of the army to which Guynemer belonged, had brought to the Guynemer family the twenty-sixth citation of their hero, the famous document which all French schoolboys have since learned by heart and which was as follows:

Fallen on the field of honour on September 11, 1917. A legendary hero, fallen from the very zenith of victory after three years' hard and continuous fighting. He will be considered the most perfect embodiment of the national qualities for his indomitable energy and perseverance and his exalted gallantry. Full of invincible belief in victory, he has bequeathed to the French soldier an imperishable memory which must add to his self-sacrificing spirit and will surely give rise to the noblest emulation.

On the motion of M. Lasies, in a session which reminded us of the great days of August, 1914, the Chamber decided on October 19 that the name of Captain Guynemer should be graven on the walls of the Pantheon. Two letters, to follow below, were read by M. Lasies, to whom they had been written. One came from Lieutenant Raymond, temporary commandant of the Storks, and was as follows:

Having the honour to command Escadrille 3 in the absence of Captain Heurtaux, still wounded in hospital, I am anxious to thank you, in the name of the few surviving Storks, for what you are doing for the memory of Guynemer.

He was our friend as well as our chief and teacher, our pride and our flag, and his loss will be felt more than any that has thinned our ranks so far.

Please be sure that our courage has not been laid low with him; our revenge will be merciless and victorious. May Guynemer's noble soul remember us fighting our aerial battles, that we may keep alight the flame he bequeathed to us.
Raymond
Commanding Escadrille 3

The other letter came from Major Brocard:

My dear Comrade:
I am profoundly moved to hear of the thought you have had of giving the highest consecration to Guynemer's memory by a ceremony at the Pantheon.

It had occurred to all of us that only the lofty dome of the Pantheon was large enough for such wings.

The poor boy fell in the fullness of triumph, with his face towards the enemy. A few days before he had sworn to me that the Germans should never take him alive. His heroic death is not more glorious than that of the gunner defending his gun, the infantryman rushing out of his trench, or even that of the poor soldier perishing in the bogs. But Guynemer was known to all. There were few who had not seen him in the sky, whether blue or cloudy, bearing on his frail linen wings some of their own faith, their own dreams, and all that their souls could hold of trust and hope.

It was for them all, whether infantrymen or gunners or pioneers, that he fought with the bitter hatred he felt for the invader, with his youthful daring and the joys of his triumphs. He knew that the battle would end fatally for him, no doubt, but knowing also that his war-bird was the instrument of saving thousands of lives, and seeing that his example called forth the noblest imitation, he remained true to his idea of self-sacrifice which he had formed a long time before, and which he saw develop with perfect calm.

Full of modesty as a soldier, but fully conscious of the greatness of his duties, he possessed the national qualities of endurance, perseverance, indifference to danger, and to these he added a most generous heart.

During his short life he had not time enough to learn bitterness, or suffering, or disillusionment.

He passed straight from the school where he was learning the history of France to where he himself could add another page to it. He went to the war driven by a mysterious power which I respect as death or genius ought to be respected.

He was a powerful thought living in a body so delicate that I, who lived so close beside him, knew it would some day be slain by the thought.

The poor boy! Other boys from every French school wrote to him every day. He was their legendary ideal, and they felt all his emotions, sharing his joys as well as his dangers. To them he was the living copy of the heroes whose exploits they read in their books. His name is constantly on their lips, for they love him as they have been taught to love the purest glories of France.

Monsieur le député, gain admittance for him to the Pantheon, where he has already been placed by the mothers and children of France. There his protecting wings will not be out of place, for under that dome where sleep those who gave us our France, they will be the symbol of those who have defended her for us.

Major Brocard

These letters roused the enthusiasm of the Chamber, and the following resolution was passed by acclamation:

The government shall have an inscription placed in the Pantheon to perpetuate the memory of Captain Guynemer, the symbol of France's highest aspirations.

On November 5 the foregoing letters were solemnly read aloud in every school, and Guynemer was presented as an example to all French schoolboys.

* * * * * * * *

The army then prepared to celebrate Guynemer as a leader, and in default of any place suitable for such a ceremony they selected the camp of Saint-Pol-sur-Mer, whence Guynemer had started on his last flight. On November 30 General Anthoine, commanding the First Army, before leaving the Flemish British sector where he had so brilliantly assisted in the success, decided to associate his men with the glorification of Guynemer.

The ceremony took place at ten in the morning. A raw breeze was blowing off the sea, whose violence the dam, raised to protect the landing-ground, was not sufficient to break. In front of the battalion which had been sent to render the military honours, waved the colours of the twenty regiments that had fought in the Flemish battles, glorious flags bearing the marks of war, some of them almost in rags. To the left, in front of the airmen, two slight figures were visible, one in black, one in horizon blue: Captain Heurtaux still on his crutches, the other *sous-lieutenant* Fonck. The former was to be made an officer, the latter a chevalier in the Legion of Honour. Heurtaux, a fair-haired, delicate, almost girlish young man, but so phenomenally self-possessed in danger, had been, as we have said, our Roland's Oliver, his companion of old days, his rival and his confidant. Fonck, whom I called Aymerillot because of his smallness, his boyish simplicity and his daring, the hope of the morrow and already a glorious soldier, had perhaps avenged Guynemer's death already. For Lieutenant Weissman, according to the *Kölnische Zeitung*, had boasted in a letter to his people of having brought down the most famous French aviator. "Don't be afraid on my account," he added, "I shall never meet such a dangerous enemy again."

Now, on September 30 Fonck had shot this Lieutenant Weissman through the head as the latter was piloting a Rumpler machine above the French lines.

While the band was playing the *Marseillaise*, accompanied by the roaring of the gale and of the sea, as well as of the aeroplanes circling above, General Anthoine stepped out in front of the row of flags. His powerful frame seemed to suggest the cuirass of the knights of old, as, silhouetted against the cloudy sky, he towered above the two diminutive aviators near whom he was standing. The band stopped playing, and the general spoke, his voice rising and falling in the wind, and swelling to a higher pitch when the elements were too rebellious. He was speaking almost on the spot where Guynemer had departed from the soil of his own country on his final flight. He said:

> I have not summoned you to pay Guynemer the last homage he has a right to from the First Army, over a coffin or a grave. No trace could be found in Poelcapelle of his mortal remains, as if the heavens, jealous of their hero, had not consented to return to earth what seems to belong to it by right, and as if Guynemer had disappeared in empyrean glory through a miraculous assumption. Therefore we shall omit, on this spot from which he soared into Infinity, the sorrowful rites generally concluding the lives of mortals, and shall merely proclaim the immortality of the Knight of the Air, without fear or reproach.
>
> Men come and go, but France remains. All who fall for her bequeath to her their own glory, and her splendour is made up of their worth. Happy is he who enriches the com-

monwealth by the complete gift of himself. Happy then the child of France whose superhuman destiny we are celebrating! Glory be to him in the heavens where he reigned supreme, and glory be to him on the earth, in our soldiers' hearts and in these flags, sacred emblems of honour and of the worship of France!

Ye flags of the second aeronautical unit and of the First Army, you keep in the mystery of your folds the memory of virtue, devotion, and sacrifice of every kind, to hand down to future generations the treasures of our national traditions!

Flags, the souls of our heroes live in you, and when your fluttering silk is heard, it is indeed their voice bidding us go from the same dangers to the same triumphs!

Flags, keep the soul of Guynemer forever. Let it raise up and multiply heroes in his likeness! Let it exalt to resolution the hearts of neophytes eager to avenge the martyr by imitating his lofty example, and let it give them power to revive the prowess of this legendary hero!

For the only homage he expects from his companions is the continuation of his work.

In the brief moment during which dying men see, as in a vision, the whole past and the whole future, if Guynemer knew a comfort it was the certainty that his comrades would successfully complete what he had begun.

You, his friends and rivals, I know well; I know that, like Guynemer, you can be trusted, that you meet bravely the formidable task he has bequeathed to you, and that you will fulfil the hopes which France had reposed in him.

It is to confirm this certitude in presence of our flags, brought to witness it, that I am glad to confer on two of his companions, two of our bravest fighters, distinctions which are at the same time a reward for the past and an earnest of future glory.

Then the general gave the accolade and embraced Heurtaux, now less dependent on his crutches, and Fonck, suddenly grown taller, children of glory, both of them, and still pale from the emotion caused by the evocation of their friend's glory. He pinned the badges on their coats. After this he added, in a lull of the conflicting elements:

Let us raise our hearts in respectful and grateful admiration for the hero whom the First Army can never forget, of whom it was so proud, and whose memory will always live in History.

Dead though he be, a man like Guynemer guides us, if we know how to follow him, along the triumphal way which, over ruins, tombs, and sacrifices, leads to victory the good and the strong.

Of itself, thanks to this religious conclusion of the general's ode, the ceremony had assumed a sort of sacred character, and the word which concludes prayers, the Amen of the officiating priest, naturally came to our lips while the general saluted with his sword the invisible spirit of the hero, and the blasts of the bugles rose above the gale and the sea.

CHAPTER 6

In the Pantheon

In the Pantheon crypt, destined, as the inscription says, for the burial of great men, the name of Guynemer will be graven on a marble slab cemented in the wall. The proper inscription for this slab will be the young soldier's last citation:

Fallen on the field of honour on September 11, 1917. A legendary hero, fallen from the very zenith of victory after three years' hard and continuous fighting. He will be considered the most perfect embodiment of the national qualities for his indomitable energy and perseverance and his exalted gallantry. Full of invincible belief in victory, he has bequeathed to the French soldier an imperishable memory which must add to his self-sacrificing spirit and will surely give rise to the noblest emulation.

"To deserve such a citation and die!" exclaimed a young officer after reading it.

In his poem, *Le Vol de la Marseillaise*, Rostand shows us the twelve Victories seated at the Invalides around the tomb of the Emperor rising to welcome their sister, the Victory of the Marne. At the Pantheon, in the crypt where they rest, Marshal Lannes and General Marceau, Lazare Carnot, the organizer of victory, and Captain La Tour d'Auvergne will rise in their turn on this young man's entrance. Victor Hugo, who is there too, will recognize at once one of the knights in his *Légende des Siècles*, and Berthelot will look upon his coming as an evidence of the fervour of youth for France as well as for science. But of them all, Marceau, his elder brother, killed at twenty-seven, will be the most welcoming.

191

Travelling in the Rhine Valley some ten or twelve years ago, I made a pilgrimage to Marceau's tomb, outside Coblenz, just above the Moselle. In a little wood stands a black marble pyramid with the following inscription in worn-out gilt letters:

Here lieth Marceau, a soldier at sixteen, a general at twenty-two, who died fighting for his country the last day of the year IV of the Republic. Whoever you may be, friend or foe, respect the ashes of this hero.

The French prisoners who died in 1870-71 at the camp of Petersberg have been buried, on the same spot. Marceau was not older than these soldiers, who died without fame or glory, when his brief and wonderful career came to an end. Without knowing it, the Germans had completed the hero's mausoleum by laying these remains around it; for it is proper that beside the chief should be represented the anonymous multitude without whom there would be no chiefs.

In 1889 the remains of Marceau were transferred to the Pantheon in Paris, and the Coblenz monument now commemorates only his name. It will be the same with Guynemer, whose remains will never be found, as if the earth had refused to engulf them; they will never be brought back, amidst the acclamations of the people, to the mount once dedicated to Saint Genevieve. But his legendary life was fitly crowned by the mystery of such a death.

One of the frescoes of Puvis de Chavannes in the Pantheon, the last to the left, represents an old woman leaning over a stone terrace and gazing at the town beneath her with its moonlit roofs and its surrounding plain, looking bluish in the night. The city is asleep, but the holy woman watches and prays. She stands tall and upright as a lily. Her lamp, which is seen at the entrance of her house, is one long stem illuminated by the flame. She, too, is like this lamp. Her emaciated body would be nothing without her ardent face. Her serenity can only come from work well done and confidence in the future. Lutetia, represented in this picture by Genevieve, is not anxious; yet she listens as if she might hear once more the threatening approach of Attila. It is because she knows that the barbarians may come back again, and can only be stopped by invincible faith.

As long as France keeps her belief, she is secure. The life and death of a Guynemer are an act of faith in immortal France.

Envoi

The *ballades* of olden times used to conclude with an *envoi* addressed to some powerful person and invariably beginning with King, Queen, Prince or Princess. But the poet was occasionally at a loss, for, as Theodore de Banville observes in his *Petit traité de Poésie Française*, "everybody has not a prince handy to whom to dedicate his *ballade.*"

Guynemer's biography is of such a nature that it must seem like a poem: why not, then, conclude it with an *envoi*? I have no difficulty in finding a Prince, for I shall select him from among the French schoolboys. There is a little Paul Bailly, not quite twelve years old, from Bouclans, a village in Franche-Comté, who wrote a beautiful theme on Guynemer: he shall be my Prince. And through him I shall address all the French schoolboys or girls, in all the French towns and villages. Little Prince, I have no doubt that you love arithmetic, and I will give you accurate figures which will satisfy your taste. You will like to know that Guynemer flew for 665 hours and 55 seconds in all, which I added up from his flying notebooks: his last flight is not recorded in them, because it never stopped.

As for the number of fights in which he was engaged, that is difficult to ascertain. Guynemer himself did not seem anxious to be sure about it. But it must be more than 600, and might well be 700 or 800. Your Guynemer, our Guynemer, will never be surpassed: not because he forgot to hand over to his successors, rivals, and avengers the sacred flame which in France can never go out, but because genius is an exceptional privilege, and because the present methods of fighting in the air are not in favour of single combats but engage whole units.

You will also love to hear about Guynemer as an inventor, and the creator of a magic aeroplane. Some day this aeroplane will be exhibited; and perhaps some of your little friends have already seen at the Invalides the machine in which Guynemer brought down nineteen German aeroplanes. On November 1, 1917, thousands of Parisians visited it; and it was strewn with magnificent bunches of chrysanthemums, to which many people added clusters of violets.

In Guynemer the technician and the marksman equalled and perhaps surpassed the pilot. Captain Galliot, who is a specialist, has called him "the thinker-fighter," thereby emphasizing that his excellence as a gunner arose from meditation and preparation. The same officer adds that "accuracy was Guynemer's characteristic; he never shot at random as others occasionally do, but always took long and careful aim. Perfect weapons and perfect mastery of them were dogmas with him. His marksmanship, the result of perseverance and intelligence, multiplied tenfold the capacity of his machine-gun, and accounts for his overwhelming superiority."[31]

But when you have realized the technical superiority of our Guynemer, you will have yet to learn one thing, one great thing, the essential thing. You have heard that Guynemer's frame was not robust; that he was delicate, and the military boards refused him several times as unfit. Yet no aviator ever showed more endurance than he did, even when developments made long cruising necessary in altitudes of 6000 or 7000 metres. There have been pilots as quick-witted and gunners as accurate as Guynemer, but there has never been anybody who equalled him in the flash-like rapidity of his attack, or for doggedness in keeping up a fight. We must conclude that he had a special gift, and this gift—his own genius—must be ultimately reduced to his decision, that is, his will-power. His will, to the very end, was far above his physical strength. There are two great dates in his short life: November 21, 1914, when he joined the army, and September 11, 1917, when he left camp for his last flight. Neither a passion for aviation nor thirst for glory had any part in his action on those two dates. Will-power in itself is sometimes dangerous, enviable though it be, and must be wisely directed. Now, Guynemer regulated his will by one great object, which was to serve, to serve his country, even unto death.

31: *Guerre aérienne*, October 18, 1917.

Finally, do not place Guynemer apart from his comrades: even in his grave, even in the region where there is no grave, he would resent it. I hope you will learn by heart the names of the French aces, at any rate those names which I am going to give you, whatever may become of those who bear them:[32]

Sous-Lieutenant Nungesser	30 aeroplanes brought down
Captain Heurtaux	21 aeroplanes brought down
Lieutenant Deullin	17 aeroplanes brought down
Lieutenant Pinsard	16 aeroplanes brought down
Sous-Lieutenant Madon	16 aeroplanes brought down
Sous-Lieutenant Chaput	12 aeroplanes brought down
Adjutant Jailler	12 aeroplanes brought down
Sous-Lieutenant Ortoli	11 aeroplanes brought down
Sous-Lieutenant Tarascon	11 aeroplanes brought down
Chief Adjutant Fonck	11 aeroplanes brought down
Sous-Lieutenant Lufbery	10 aeroplanes brought down

These names will become more and more glorious—some have already done so—and others will be added to the list which you will learn also. But however tenacious your memory may be, you will never remember, nobody will ever remember, the thousands of names we ought to save from oblivion, the names of those whose patience, courage, and sufferings have saved the soil of France. The fame of one man is nothing unless it represent the obscure deeds of the anonymous multitude. The name of Guynemer ought to sum up the sacrifice of all French youth—infantrymen, gunners, pioneers, troopers, or flyers—who have given their lives for us, as we hear the infinite murmur of the ocean in one beautiful shell.

The enthusiasm and patience, the efforts and sacrifices, of the generations which came before you, little boy, were necessary to save you, to save your country, to save the world, born of light and born unto light, from the darkness of dread oppression. Germany has chosen to rob war of all that, slowly and tentatively, the nations had given to it of respect for treaties, pity for the weak and defenceless, and of honour generally. She has poisoned it as she poisons her gases. This is what we should never forget. Not only has Germany forced this war upon the world, but she has made it systematically cruel and terrifying, and in so doing she has sown

32: List made September 11, 1917.

the seeds of horrified rebellion against anything that is German. Parisian boys of your own age will tell you that during their sleep German squadrons used to fly over their city dropping bombs at random upon it. And to what purpose? None, beyond useless murder. This is the kind of war which Germany has waged from the first, gradually compelling her opponents to adopt the same methods. But while this loathsome work was being done, our aeroplanes, piloted by soldiers not much older than you, cruised like moving stars above the city of Genevieve, threatened now with unheard-of invasion from on high.

Little boy, do not forget that this war, blending all classes, has also blended in a new crucible all the capacities of our country. They are now turned against the aggressor, but they will have to be used in time for union, love, and peace. *Omne regnum divisum contra se desolabitur; et omnis civitas vel domus divisa contra se non stabit.* You can read this easy Latin, but if necessary your teacher or village priest will help you. The house, the city, the nation ought not to be divided. The enemy would have done us too much evil if he had not brought about the reconciliation of all Frenchmen. You, little boy, will have to wipe away the blood from the bleeding face of France, to heal her wounds, and secure for her the revival she will urgently need. She will come out of the formidable contest respected and admired, but oh, how weary! Love her with pious love, and let the life of Guynemer inspire you with the resolve to serve in daily life, as he served, even unto death.

Genealogy of Georges Guynemer

In *Huon de Bordeaux*, a *chanson de geste* with fairy and romantic elements, Huon leaves for Babylon on a mission confided to him by the Emperor, which he was told to fulfil with the aid of the dwarf sorcerer, Oberon. At the château of Dunôtre, in Palestine, where he must destroy a giant, he meets a young girl of great beauty named Sébile, who guides him through the palace. As he is astonished to hear her speak French, she replies:

"I was born in France, and I felt pity for you because I saw the cross you wear."

"In what part of France?"

"In the town of Saint-Omer," replied Sébile; "I am the daughter of Count Guinemer." Her father had lately come on a pilgrimage to the Holy Sepulchre, bringing her with him. A tempest had cast them on shore near the town of the giant, who had killed her father and kept her prisoner. "For more than seven years," she added, "I have not been to mass." Naturally Huon kills the giant, and delivers the daughter of Count Guinemer.

In an article by the learned M. Longnon on *L'Elément historique de Huon de Bordeaux*,[33] a note is given on the name of Guinemer:

> In *Huon de Bordeaux* the author of the *Prologue des Lorrains* makes Guinemer the son of Saint Bertin, second Abbot of Sithieu, an abbey which took the name of this blessed man and was the foundation of the city of Saint-Omer, which the poem of *Huon de Bordeaux* makes the birthplace of Count Guinemer's daughter. It is possible that this Guine-

---

33: *Romania*, 1879, p. 4.

mer was borrowed by our *trouveres* from some ancient Walloon tradition; for his name, which in Latin is Winemarus, appears to have occurred chiefly in those countries forming part, from the ninth to the twelfth century, of the County of Flanders. The chartulary of Saint Vertin alone introduces us to:

1st, a deacon named Winidmarus, who in 723 wrote a deed of sale at Saint-Omer itself

2nd, a knight of the County of Flanders, Winemarus, who assassinated the Archbishop of Rheims, Foulques, who was then Abbot of Saint-Bertin

3rd, Winemarus, a vassal of the Abbey, mentioned in an act dated 1075

4th, Winemarus, Lord of Gand, witness to a charter of Count Baudouin VII in 1114

The personage in *Huon de Bordeaux* might also be connected with Guimer, Lord of Saint-Omer, who appears in the beginning of *Ogier le Danios*, if the form, Guimer, did not seem rather to derive from Withmarus.[34]

Leaving the *chansons de geste*, Guinemer reappears in the history of the Crusades. Count Baudouin of Flanders and his knights, while making war in the Holy Land (1097), see a vessel approaching, more than three miles from the city of Tarsus. They wait on the shore, and the vessel casts anchor. "Whence do you come?" is always the first question asked in like circumstances. "From Flanders, from Holland, and from Friesland." They were repentant pirates, who after having combed the seas had come to do penance by a pilgrimage to Jerusalem. The Christian warriors joyously welcome these sailors whose help will be useful to them. Their chief is a Guinemer, not from Saint-Omer but Boulogne. He recognizes in Count Baudouin his liege lord, leaves his ship and decides to remain with the crusaders. "*Moult*

34: With this note may be connected the following page of the Wauters, a chronological table of Charters and printed Acts, Vol. II, p. 16, 1103: "Baldéric, Bishop of the Tournaisiens and the Noyonnais, confirms the cession of the tithe and patronage of Templeuve, which was made to the Abbey of Saint-Martin de Tournai by two knights of that town, Arnoul and Guinemer, and by the canon *Géric. Actum Tornaci, anno domenice incarnationis M.C. III, regnante rege Philippo, episcopante domo Baldrico pontifice.* Extracts for use in the ecclesiastic history of Belgium, 2nd year."

estait riche de ce mauvais gaeng." The whilom pirate contributes his ill-gotten gains to the crusade.[35]

In another chapter of the *Histoire des Croisades*, this Guinemer besieged Lalische, which "is a most noble and ancient city situated on the border of the sea; it was the only city in Syria over which the Emperor of Constantinople was ruler." Lalische or Laodicea in Syria, *Laodicea ad mare*—now called Latakia—was an ancient Roman colony under Septimus Severus, and was founded on the ruins of the ancient Ramitha by Seleucus Nicator, who called it Laodicea in honour of his mother Laodice. Guinemer, who expected to take the city by force, was in his turn assaulted and taken prisoner by the garrison. Baudouin, with threats, demanded him back and rescued him; but esteeming him a better seaman than a combatant on the land, he invited him to return to his ship, take command of his fleet, and navigate within sight of the coast, which the former pirate "very willingly did."

A catalogue of the Deeds of Henri I, King of France (1031-1060)[36] mentions in this same period a Guinemer, Lord of Lillers, who had solicited the approval of the king for the construction of a church in his château, to be dedicated to Notre-Dame and Saint-Omer. The royal approval was given in 1043, completing the authorization of Baudouin, Count of Flanders, and of Dreu, Bishop of Thérouanne at the request of Pope Gregory VI, to whom the builder had gone in person to ask consent for his enterprise. Was this Guinemer, like the pirate of Jerusalem, doing penance for some wrong? Thus we find two Guinemers in the eleventh century, one in Palestine, the other in Italy. About this same period the family probably left Flanders to settle in Brittany, where they remained until the Revolution. The corsair of Boulogne became a ship-builder at Saint-Malo, having his own reasons for changing parishes. The Flemish tradition then gives place to that of Brittany, which is authenticated by documents. One Olivier Guinemer gave a receipt in 1306 to the executors of Duke Jean II de Bretagne. He held a fief under Saint-Sauveur de Dinan, "on which the duke had settled tenants contrary to agreements." The executors, to liquidate

---

35: *Receuil des Historiens des Croisades*, Western Historians, Volume I, Book III and XXIII, p. 145: *Comment Guinemerz et il Galiot s'accompaignierent avec Baudouin.* Footnote 36: *Catalogue des actes d'Henri I, Roi de France* (1031-1060), by Frédéric Soehnée, archivist at the National Archives.

the estate, had to pay immense sums for "indemnification, restitution and damages," and took care to "take receipts from all those to whom their commission obliged them to distribute money."[37] The Treaty of Guérande (April 11, 1365), which ended the war for the Breton succession and gave the Duchy to Jean de Montfort, though under the suzerainty of the King of France, is signed by thirty Breton knights, among whom is a Geoffrey Guinemer. A Mathelin Guinemer, squire, is mentioned in an act received at Bourges in 1418; while in 1464, an Yvon Guynemer, man-at-arms, is promoted to full pay, and he already spells his name with a y.

It is somewhat difficult to trace the history of this lesser provincial nobility, engaged sometimes in petty wars, sometimes in the cultivation of their domains. In a book glorifying the humble service of ancient French society, Gentilshommes Campagnards, M. Pierre de Vaissiére has shown how this race of rural proprietors lived in the closest contact with French agriculture, counseling and defending the peasant, clearing and cultivating their land, and maintaining their families by its produce. In his Mémoires, the famous Rétif de la Bretonne paints in the most picturesque manner the patriarchal and authoritative manners of his grandfather who, by virtue of his own unquestioned authority prevented his descendant from leaving his native village and establishing in Paris. Paris was already exercising its fascination and uprooting the youth of the time. The Court of Versailles had already weakened the social authority of families still attached to their lands.

Footnote 37: *Histoire de Bretagne*, by Dom Lobineau (1707), Vol. I, p. 293. *Recherches sur la chevalerie du duché de Bretagne*, by A. de Couffon de Kerdellech, Vol. II (Nantes, Vincent Forest and Emile Grimaud, Printers and Publishers).

The Chevalier of Flight

by Mary R. Parkman

A hero of legendary power, he fell in the wide heaven of glory, after three years of hard fighting. He will long remain the purest symbol of the qualities of the race: indomitable in tenacity, enthusiastic in energy, sublime in courage. Animated with inextinguishable faith in victory, he bequeaths to the French soldier the imperishable remembrance which will exalt the spirit of sacrifice and the most noble emulation.

Inscription to Guynemer in the Pantheon

Of all the heroes of the World War, Georges Guynemer, the "gallant flying boy" of France, most appeals to the imagination. "A hero of legendary power, he fell in the wide heaven of glory after three years of hard fighting" reads the inscription set up in his memory in the Pantheon, that classic Hall of Heroes in Paris. The very sound of his name enkindles ardor and stirs the heart. He has been called "the knight of the air," "the winged sword of France," and the story of his miraculous exploits is already linked with that of Joan of Arc. Like her, he seems to stand for the eager, unquench-able spirit of France. He was born on Christmas Eve, 1894. "I lead a charmed life," he used to say laughingly when his companions protested that he took too many risks. "You see it is not easy to hurt a chap who was born on Christmas Eve!"

He was a child of frail body and indomitable will. It was as if Fate sought to prove once and for all that spirit was master—that soul could conquer in spite of every physical handicap. See the picture of him, a lad of twelve, among his mates at school. He is slighter and paler than them all, but his dark eyes burn with an intense fire that defies all restraint, all fettering bonds of bodily limitation, and even, we can fancy, knowing the story of the triumph of his brief life, the mortal exactions of Time and Space....

As a tiny lad, he knew that his parents had grave concern be-cause of his health. There were many consultations with physicians; there were journeys in search of health and strength. His education began at home under the governess of his two sisters.

"No doubt it is best," complained his father, a retired army of-ficer, whose fondest dream it was that his only son should win a place among those who serve their country, "but it looks as if we may have one petticoat too many in the family."

There were walks with the father, and many long talks about the glories of the past that their town of Compeigne had shared. The chief enthusiasm of Guynemer *pere* was history, and there was not one of the streets where they walked but could furnish a text. Kings had been consecrated there; kings had died there. Treaties that changed the destiny of nations had been signed there. Louis the Grand and the great Napoleon had given splendid fetes there. . . . But every walk to the palace, the abbey, or to the forest, was somehow incomplete if they did not go by the open square of the Hotel-de-ville, where a maiden in armour stood lifting the standard of France to the sky.

"Who is she?" asked the child.

"Jeanne d'Arc."

Again and again he stood there gazing at the figure of the young girl who had led the armies of her country to victory and crowned her king, as he demanded to hear yet again about the miracle of her short life. It appeared that history was not all made by the wise and prudent like his father, but that children, too, had been able to do glorious things. Something seemed to draw him to that bronze maiden, who stood there straight as a sword, bearing her banner aloft. His heart burned within him, and a whisper came that guided all his days.

"It is not how long we live that matters, but how and what we live. Life is not measured by the clock, but by noble heart-beats and brave deeds." . . . The thought became clearer each time he stopped before the statue of the Maid. Surely she had lived as much for herself and the world as any one, no matter how many years and honours he might have to his credit.

When his father told him the stories of his own people—how there was a Guynemer among those about whom the poet sang in the "Song of Roland," that men of that name had been among those who fared forth on tlie Crusades, and that ever since, his forbears had been men who had served their country gallantly, keeping the honour of their fine, old family bright, again the whisper came, "It is not how long they lived that counts. Who cares to know the age of a Roland? The memory of glorious deeds alone remains."

At the age of twelve, little Georges Guynemer entered Stanislas College at Compeigne as a day pupil. They tell us that he was no book-worm —that he was too "tameless and swift and proud" to be held down by routine exercises. His quickness of intelligence and ready wit were recognized, and his "ambition of the first rank." At the end of the first year, Georges had won first prize in arithmetic, but it was on the playground in games that demanded agility and daring that the slight boy most distinguished himself.

One game known as *la petite guerre* delighted the boy above everything else. The group of boys was divided into two armies, each commanded by a general chosen by themselves. All the soldiers strove to defend bands of colour which they wore as armlets, and also to preserve from capture flags which floated from a wall, tree, or some other selected spot. A boy whose armlet was seized was *hors de combat*—a dead soldier. It is interesting to note that the boy who was most lacking in physical strength was a leader in this game. His energy, quickness of eye and wit, as well as his darting swiftness of movement and daring originality of attack, won for him first place. But it is to be noted also that he was never chosen general. His gifts were too much needed in the ranks of those who fought, and besides, he loved the struggle for its own sake. How he delighted in attacking the strongest and the most distinguished scholars of them all, conquering by a sudden turn before the other could tell what was happening;—and then the triumph of bearing the trophies to his general! He had no desire for leadership that would give him a role apart and aloof, leaving to others the chances and thrills that belong to the heat of the fray. So Georges Guynemer was always *simple soldat*.

We have here an astonishing likeness of the youth, who, a few years later, was chief among all his country's brave knights of the air, the ace of aces who had fifty-four aeroplanes and two hundred and fifteen combats to his credit. He cared too much for the fight to wish to command. He was the knight of solitary combat, preferring even to go alone in his machine, which he controlled with his feet and one hand while he fired his gun with the other. He attacked always the strongest, daunted neither by the number nor prowess of his antagonists. His quickness and unexpectedness of attack were unequalled. As if to show that life did not depend upon brawn or upon any virtue of physique alone, he conquered in spite of his frail body, proving that the will to do can triumph over every obstacle and overthrow the strongest.

Notwithstanding periods of enforced retirement from his studies to the infirmary, or to his home for a prolonged rest of two or three months, he succeeded in keeping abreast of his class and in graduating at the age of fifteen. The next autumn he returned to go on with his studies in preparation for the Polytechnic, specializing in mathematics and physics. At the same time his native interest in mechanics engaged not only most of his spare time but also many hours stolen from his regular tasks. His room was a veritable curiosity shop, where coils of wire, wheels, chemicals, batteries, and all sorts of mechanical odds and ends were jumbled together with note-books, staid texts, and articles of clothing.

His spirit of invention which had shown itself when he was a child of four or five, now came into play in constructing a telephone that should put him in quick communication with a friend in a distant part of the building. He developed a passion for experimentation in physics and chemistry.

"He was absorbed for hours at a time," said Lieutenant Constantin, a comrade at Stanislas, "in working over problems in mathematics or mechanics, without giving a thought to what went on around. When he had solved the problem that challenged him or had succeeded in discovering something new, he would return satisfied to the affairs of the moment."

A friendship made during these days at school had a great influence on the particular development of his interests. Jean Krebs, son of the manager of the Panhard motor car factory—that Colonel Krebs whose name is associated with the early progress in the production of aerial motors —became young Guynemer's constant companion. The workshop of his room or even the college laboratory was too narrow now. His real school was the motor factory, where he eagerly mastered the fascinating details of workmanship and management of the various engines and mechanical contrivances.

One day during the last year of preparation for the Polytechnic, his father carried him off for a much-needed rest to his grandmother's in Paris, after which he spent some weeks in travel with his mother and sisters. Then, one day, his father drew him apart for a serious talk.

"You have had, my son, your years of preparatory study, and some leisure to think of the future. What profession do you plan to follow?"

Without a moment's pause or change of expression, as if he were not aware of saying something extraordinary, Georges replied, "Aviator."

"But that is not a profession," said the amazed father. "That is only a sport. You run through the air as an *automobilist* chases along the highways of the country. Then after spending your best years in the pursuit of pleasure, where are you?"

Then Georges told his father what he had not breathed before to a living soul, not even his friend, Constantin, or Jean Krebs. "I have no other passion. One morning from the quadrangle of the college I saw an aviator fly over high in the air. I cannot explain what happened, but something new took possession of me. I felt a deeper emotion than I have ever known before, a feeling almost religious. You must trust me, my father, when I beg you to let me go with the aeroplanes."

"You do not know what it is that you ask, my boy," replied the father, moved by his son's extraordinary earnestness. "You have no knowledge of a flying machine except from below. It is a far-away romance to you."

"You are wrong," replied Georges, "I have been up in one at Corbeaulieu." Corbeaulieu was an aerodrome not far from Compeigne.

A few months later, in July, 1914, the Guynemers were at Biarritz. Much had happened in the intervening weeks. Georges had been denied admission to the Polytechnic because of his frail health.

"He will not live to complete the course," declared the examining professors. It was the first real disappointment of the boy's life— the first closed door. Heretofore he had not felt that his weak body was a particular handicap; his spirit had risen triumphant over every limitation. But now it appeared that others had the power to rule for him, and to prevent his entering the life he felt must be his.

To Biarritz they went for the mellow sunshine and soft sea

breezes of the famous resort. Surely such golden days would bring health and strength. There were, however, other possibilities besides loitering on the sands and bathing at Biarritz. The beach made a fine landing-place for aeroplanes. It was not accident, you may be sure, that brought young Guynemer to the spot when one of the great birds swept down to earth. He examined the motor and every detail of the machine; he talked to the pilot. He never doubted that he was born to fly!

But then, as in a day, the gay world of study and adventure was changed. A heavy cloud obscured the sunshine even at Biarritz. His country was plunged in war. In a moment former dreams and longings passed away with the sunshine. Even flying was forgotten as something unreal and far away. Georges stood before his father, breathless with suspense.

"I must enlist," he said.

"It is your right," replied the ex-captain, looking at his son proudly.

"You will permit—"

"I envy you," was the firm answer.

But again a closed door! Three times the youth presented himself, and three times he was refused. They could not see beyond the slight form and the delicate chest, and recognize the spirit that would push on and triumph in real warfare for his country, as the frail child had overcome the strongest at school in the game of war. He felt that life held nothing for him; it seemed that he was helpless to lift himself out of the slough of despond.

Then, one day, a glimpse of his old friend, the gallant Maid who stood as ever, holding aloft the standard of her country, quickened his spirit. She, too, had known the torture of feeling herself held back when all her soul was urging her forward, but she had kept on and saved France. It was not always by strength and might that destiny was shaped. . . . Some solemn words that he had heard chanted in church rang in his ears now with new meaning:

He hath put down the mighty
And hath exalted the humble and meek.

Was not Joan of Arc an eternal witness to the truth of those words?

As in a flash he saw what he could do. His old dreams revived in a new guise, and he saw the path ahead. He was on the sand when an aeroplane came to earth that day, and he talked earnestly for a moment with the sergeant-pilot.

"How does one enlist in the aviation service?" he asked.

"See the Captain at Pau," was the reply.

The boy's parents hardly recognized him when he next appeared, his face alight with life and hope. Surely the doctors were mistaken; he must get well. It was unthinkable that such youth and fire should be so soon extinguished.

"*Mon pere*, I must go to Pau to-morrow," he declared without preamble, "to enlist as an aviator. Before the war you would not listen, but now you see that aviation is more than a sport." And the hid had his wish. On the morrow he presented himself before Captain Bernard-Thierry, who was in command of the aviation camp at Pau. It seemed as if his heart would burst, and the eager words fairly tripped over each other.

"My Captain, do me but this favour. Take me in! Employ me at anything at all, even cleaning the machines. You are my last chance. Let it be through you that I am permitted to do something in this war."

The Captain looked at the slender boy with the burning eyes and flushed cheeks. He saw more than the slight form; he divined something of the power of the spirit within. He was a man who believed that the soul is master of the frame in which it dwells.

"I can take you as pupil-mechanic," he said.

Guynemer drew a long sigh. This door at least was not shut. "Good!" he exulted. "I have some knowledge of motors."

That was in November, 1914. After two months as mechanic he had won a place among the ranks of student aviators, and on February first he made his trial trip aloft as pilot. "I began in a 'taxi' " he said, "and then the following week I mounted an airplane, going in straight lines, turning and gliding; and on March 10 I made two flights lasting twenty minutes. At last I had found my wings; I passed the examination next day."

We are told that Guynemer's ambitious spirit almost proved his undoing at the very beginning of his career. The head pilot complained that he was too rash, venturing out in contrary weather and essaying turns that were far too difficult for one of his small experience. Guynemer always shivered slightly when he spoke of how narrowly he had escaped being dropped from the list of military aviators.

It was not long before the master pilot and all the rest of the camp knew that the youth they had so nearly lost was the leader of them all—an eagle among the birds of the air. Though his daring attacks seemed to take no account of risks, he returned victorious from every encounter. As the boy at school in the game of war had always sought to vanquish the strongest, so now the young eagle always marked the flight of the first among the enemy planes and strove to bring those to the ground. Before three weeks had passed, he had brought his fifth Boche plane to the earth, thus becoming an ace.

The splendid abandon and sublime courage of his adventures in the air won the adoring admiration of all his comrades, and accounts of his exploits were passed eagerly from mouth to mouth.

The story of the combat of September 29, 1916, moved all France, and the young aviator awoke to find himself the hero of the hour. Seeing one of his comrades attacked by five enemy planes, he mounted to the rescue. At a height of 10,000 feet, he shot and sent to earth two within thirty seconds of each other. The others tried to escape, but pursuing, he brought down a third in two minutes. Then—a mischief!—a shell exploded under his machine tearing off one of the wings of the noble bird. Down he fell into No Man's Land where in an instant he was seen rising from the wreck. The enemy opened up a diabolical machine gun fire to prevent his escape, but with a mighty shout the French surged "over the top" and succeeded in effecting a rescue. That was the occasion that won for Guynemer the rank of lieutenant, and the decoration of the *croix de guerre*.

Let us read one of the brief entries in his diary, for January 26, 1917. He has been attacking a Boche plane in his best manner by descending on it from above, when his gun becomes disabled.

> I try to bluff. I mount to 2000 feet over him and drop onto him like a stone. For a moment I think that was without effect when he begins to descend. I put myself ten yards behind him, but every time I showed my nose around the edge of his tail the gunner took aim at me.

We take the road towards Compeigne—3000 feet—2000 feet —again I show my nose and this time the gunner lets go his machine gun and motions to me that he surrenders. All right!

I see four bombs stowed away under his machine. 1500 feet. The Boche slows down his windmill. I swerve over him while he lands, but not having any gun or ammunition I cannot prevent the Boches from setting fire to their taxi, a 200 H. P. Albatros, magnificent. When I see that they are safely surrounded I come down and show the Boches my crippled machine gun.

If it seemed to others that he ran needless risks in the spirit of untamed adventure, he always declared that he never took random chances—that he saw his way. His extraordinary quickness of eye and movement, together with his absolute fearlessness that saved him from indecision at a critical moment, account for many of his seemingly miraculous escapes. His individual method of acting both as pilot and gunner was another source of strength; it enabled him to carry more gasoline and ammunition, and his aim was as sure as his management of his wings. The gun, which was attached to the top of the machine over his head, was controlled by a lever that could be operated with one hand. The sights were directly in front so that he aimed by pointing his machine. Guynemer, the practical machinist, was, moreover, always on duty before every flight. No one could accuse him of recklessness and say that he was saved through some magic of luck who saw him prepare for an attack. He spent an hour in carefully, lovingly, examining his aeroplane and gun. Every screw and buckle was put to the test. Every cartridge was inspected and oiled, together with all the other parts of his equipment. He knew the exact condition of his motor and propeller, and so was sure what he could count on in case of stress.

Guynemer 's squadron, "The Storks," so called from the flying stork painted on the side of each machine, included more aviators of note than any other escadrille. Fourteen members of this group brought down a third of all the German machines destroyed before January, 1918, two hundred in less than three years, according to the official count.

Among all of the famous "Storks," René Dormé was second only to Guynemer in the management of his machine and the sureness of his aim. His disappearance over the enemy lines after a fierce battle in the clouds four months before the loss of Guynemer himself, was mourned by all his comrades. On the day that he went from them, May 25, 1917, Guynemer scored his famous quadruple victory. It seemed as if the strength born of his avenging rage knew no bounds. Seeing three machines flying together toward the French lines, he made one of his spectacular mounts, swooped down upon them, and put them to flight. Pursuing, he succeeded in getting one in the line of fire and brought it to earth in flames.

The one weakness of Guynemer 's solitary method of fighting was the danger of rear attack. That was where his marvellous agility came into play—darting, turning, he seemed ready at every point. After bringing down, now, his first Boche, the avenger wheeled and saw a second trying to reach him at the moment he was intent upon his conquest; but he had already received from above one of the French explosive bullets, and in a moment fell in flames like his companion. A third Boche who dared to approach the French aviation field at noon of the same day was sighted by Guynemer, who was at the time high in the air.

Swooping down like a wrathful spirit, he fired but one shot when the rash enemy fell to earth; the bullet had found the head of the pilot. That same evening Guynemer mounted again and brought down his fourth machine in flames—a spectacular finish for his great day. It was this quadruple victory that won for Guynemer the Rosette of the Legion of Honour which was presented with this commendation:

An elite officer, a fighting pilot as skilful as audacious. He has rendered glowing service to his country, both by the number of his victories and the daily example he has set of burning ardour and even greater mastery increasing from day to day. Unconscious of danger, on account of his sureness of method and precision of manoeuvres, he has become the most redoubtable of all to the enemy. On May 25, 1917, he accomplished one of his most brilliant exploits, beating down two enemy airplanes in one minute, and gaining two more victories the same day. By all of his exploits he has contributed towards exalting the courage and enthusiasm of those, who, from the trenches, were the witnesses of his triumphs. He has brought down forty-five airplanes, received twenty citations and been seriously wounded twice.

But I think that more than any eulogy of the great or adoration of the crowd, Georges Guynemer would have hold dear this fervid tribute of little Franc-Comtois Paul Bailly, an eleven-year-old schoolboy in the village of Bouclans, who was selected by his mates to speak for them in a composition written on the day set apart for the commemoration of the life of the hero of aces in the schools:

Guynemer is the Roland of our epoch. Like Roland he was very valiant, and like Roland, he died for France. But his exploits are not a legend, like those of Roland; they are more splendid when told in simple truth than if they had been invented. For his glorification there is to be written in the Pantheon his own among the other great names. His aeroplane is placed in the Invalides. At our school a day is consecrated to him; we have his portrait on our wall; we have learned his last citation in the army orders as a lesson; we have traced his name for penmanship; and we have made a drawing of an aeroplane.

Roland was the pattern of the chevaliers of another age. Guynemer becomes the pattern of the French of to-day and all will try to follow his example. I indeed shall never forget him; I shall keep the remembrance that he, like my dear papa, died for France.

And so it was that to young and old, to the soldiers in the trenches, to workmen in the factories, and to war-weary people throughout the land, Guynemer was the incarnation of the glorious, unconquerable soul of France.

In the summer of 1917, the young hero's friends sought to prevail upon him to take some much needed rest.

"You wanted to bring down fifty; that was the goal that you set for yourself. Can you not now be satisfied for a little?" pleaded his father.

"They will think I have stopped because I have won all the honours they have to give; they will think that I fought for the prizes!" said Georges. "It is my life to fly."

"But surely now that you are the leader of the squadron you must see that you have enough work for a while in planning, in teaching and directing us all," urged his companions.

"How can you expect me to hold back and hoard myself when adventure beckons!" he replied. "Bringing down Boches is meat and drink to me."

Guynemer loved his little machine with clipped wings as Roland did his horse. Though he won his aceship in a slower model, his favourite steed could rise 10,000 feet in ten minutes and maintain the rate of 120 miles an hour. This "scorner of the ground" lost its buoyancy when the speed was less than 60 miles, and it was, therefore, necessary to bring it to a landing at that rate. How Guynemer chafed when, in the stress of a moment, he was forced to use a borrowed machine. Now his own model is kept, a sacred relic, in the Invalides.

In one of the old hero tales of the Norse we read that when the gods wished to summon Sigmund, the glorious, to the joys of Valhalla, Odin, himself, stayed his hand in the midst of battle, and broke his magic sword. We might believe that the Chevalier of Flight was singled out by the gods that August, for his marvellous power seemed all at once to pass from him. He struggled fiercely against fate—in one day flying seven hours and engaging in several encounters, but all without a single success. On September 10, the day before the last flight, he attempted to set out in three different machines, but all proved contrary and forced him back to earth. That evening his companions, despairing of making him listen to reason, telephoned to his old commanding officer to come and carry him off before he did himself a mischief. Commander Brocard wired Guynemer that he was coming to see him at nine o 'clock the next morning.

It seemed as if the young eagle divined their schemes to cage him. At eight o'clock, calling Lieutenant Bozon-Verduras to accompany him, Guynemer set out on his last flight. As in the case of the greatest heroes, his passing was shrouded in mystery. The French peasants declare that he was never brought to the ground, but that his dauntless wings carried him straight up to heaven. All that his companion could tell was this: Guynemer sighted an enemy machine and flew to the attack, leaving him to ward off a possible interference from a group of fighting planes in the distance. They turned off in another direction, however, without seeing the eagle circling above. When the lieutenant returned to his station, the eagle had passed out of sight.

"Surely," he thought, "he brought down his game and followed to see the finish."

But that was the last that was seen of the leader of the "Storks." News of his disappearance was carefully suppressed, so that his chances of escape might not be lessened in case he had been forced to land in enemy territory. But in spite of everything, a London newspaper of September 17 gave out the story of his loss, and some days after this the Cologne *Gazette* printed an item, saying casually that a pilot to fame unknown, one Wisseman, had written home that he had brought down, *on September 10*, the great ace of aces, and so could not doubt his power to conquer everywhere!

Though the Germans had always been accustomed to announce immediately the fall of an enemy aviator, this was the only news of the great Guynemer that was forthcoming for ten days after his disappearance.

Application was made through the Red Cross to Germany for official information as to the disposition of his body, and the reply came that after he had been brought down on *September 10* he was buried with military honours in the cemetery at Poelcappelle in Belgium. When this village a few days later fell into the hands of the British, however, the search for his grave was in vain. In reply to a further request for information, the news was vouchsafed that Guynemer's body could not be removed from the wreck of his machine because of the unceasing artillery fire, which finally, in flames and upturned earth destroyed every trace of the aeroplane and its pilot.

It may be that the children and the untaught peasants are right when they say that the life of the marvellous boy ended in a miracle. At any rate his fiery spirit left no cold ashes to be returned to Mother Earth, even to the sacred soil of his beloved France, when it passed into the eternal sky—fire unto fire!

On the tablet erected to his memory in the Pantheon are inscribed these words:

Captain Guynemer, commander of Squadron No. 3, died on

the field of honour September 11, 1917. A hero of legendary power, he fell in the wide heaven of glory, after three years of hard fighting. He will long remain the purest symbol of the qualities of the race: indomitable in tenacity, enthusiastic in energy, sublime in courage. Animated with inextinguishable faith in victory, he bequeaths to the French soldier the imperishable remembrance which will exalt the spirit of sacrifice and the most noble emulation.

LEONAUR

ALSO FROM LEONAUR
AVAILABLE IN SOFTCOVER OR HARDCOVER WITH DUST JACKET

AFGHANISTAN: THE BELEAGUERED BRIGADE *by G. R. Gleig*—An Account of Sale's Brigade During the First Afghan War.

IN THE RANKS OF THE C. I. V *by Erskine Childers*—With the City Imperial Volunteer Battery (Honourable Artillery Company) in the Second Boer War.

THE BENGAL NATIVE ARMY *by F. G. Cardew*—An Invaluable Reference Resource.

THE 7TH (QUEEN'S OWN) HUSSARS: Volume 4—1688-1914 *by C. R. B. Barrett*—Uniforms, Equipment, Weapons, Traditions, the Services of Notable Officers and Men & the Appendices to All Volumes—Volume 4: 1688-1914.

THE SWORD OF THE CROWN *by Eric W. Sheppard*—A History of the British Army to 1914.

THE 7TH (QUEEN'S OWN) HUSSARS: Volume 3—**1818-1914** *by C. R. B. Barrett*—On Campaign During the Canadian Rebellion, the Indian Mutiny, the Sudan, Matabeleland, Mashonaland and the Boer War Volume 3: 1818-1914.

THE KHARTOUM CAMPAIGN *by Bennet Burleigh*—A Special Correspondent's View of the Reconquest of the Sudan by British and Egyptian Forces under Kitchener—1898.

EL PUCHERO *by Richard McSherry*—The Letters of a Surgeon of Volunteers During Scott's Campaign of the American-Mexican War 1847-1848.

RIFLEMAN SAHIB *by E. Maude*—The Recollections of an Officer of the Bombay Rifles During the Southern Mahratta Campaign, Second Sikh War, Persian Campaign and Indian Mutiny.

THE KING'S HUSSAR *by Edwin Mole*—The Recollections of a 14th (King's) Hussar During the Victorian Era.

JOHN COMPANY'S CAVALRYMAN *by William Johnson*—The Experiences of a British Soldier in the Crimea, the Persian Campaign and the Indian Mutiny.

COLENSO & DURNFORD'S ZULU WAR *by Frances E. Colenso & Edward Durnford*—The first and possibly the most important history of the Zulu War.

U. S. DRAGOON *by Samuel E. Chamberlain*—Experiences in the Mexican War 1846-48 and on the South Western Frontier.

LEONAUR

ALSO FROM LEONAUR
AVAILABLE IN SOFTCOVER OR HARDCOVER WITH DUST JACKET

THE 2ND MAORI WAR: 1860-1861 *by Robert Carey*—The Second Maori War, or First Taranaki War, one more bloody instalment of the conflicts between European settlers and the indigenous Maori people.

A JOURNAL OF THE SECOND SIKH WAR *by Daniel A. Sandford*—The Experiences of an Ensign of the 2nd Bengal European Regiment During the Campaign in the Punjab, India, 1848-49.

THE LIGHT INFANTRY OFFICER *by John H. Cooke*—The Experiences of an Officer of the 43rd Light Infantry in America During the War of 1812.

BUSHVELDT CARBINEERS *by George Witton*—The War Against the Boers in South Africa and the 'Breaker' Morant Incident.

LAKE'S CAMPAIGNS IN INDIA *by Hugh Pearse*—The Second Anglo Maratha War, 1803-1807.

BRITAIN IN AFGHANISTAN 1: THE FIRST AFGHAN WAR 1839-42 *by Archibald Forbes*—From invasion to destruction-a British military disaster.

BRITAIN IN AFGHANISTAN 2: THE SECOND AFGHAN WAR 1878-80 *by Archibald Forbes*—This is the history of the Second Afghan War-another episode of British military history typified by savagery, massacre, siege and battles.

UP AMONG THE PANDIES *by Vivian Dering Majendie*—Experiences of a British Officer on Campaign During the Indian Mutiny, 1857-1858.

MUTINY: 1857 *by James Humphries*—Authentic Voices from the Indian Mutiny-First Hand Accounts of Battles, Sieges and Personal Hardships.

BLOW THE BUGLE, DRAW THE SWORD *by W. H. G. Kingston*—The Wars, Campaigns, Regiments and Soldiers of the British & Indian Armies During the Victorian Era, 1839-1898.

WAR BEYOND THE DRAGON PAGODA *by Major J. J. Snodgrass*—A Personal Narrative of the First Anglo-Burmese War 1824 - 1826.

THE HERO OF ALIWAL *by James Humphries*—The Campaigns of Sir Harry Smith in India, 1843-1846, During the Gwalior War & the First Sikh War.

ALL FOR A SHILLING A DAY *by Donald F. Featherstone*—The story of H.M. 16th, the Queen's Lancers During the first Sikh War 1845-1846.

LEONAUR

ALSO FROM LEONAUR
AVAILABLE IN SOFTCOVER OR HARDCOVER WITH DUST JACKET

ZULU:1879 *by D.C.F. Moodie & the Leonaur Editors*—The Anglo-Zulu War of 1879 from contemporary sources: First Hand Accounts, Interviews, Dispatches, Official Documents & Newspaper Reports.

THE RED DRAGOON *by W.J. Adams*—With the 7th Dragoon Guards in the Cape of Good Hope against the Boers & the Kaffir tribes during the 'war of the axe' 1843-48'.

THE RECOLLECTIONS OF SKINNER OF SKINNER'S HORSE *by James Skinner*—James Skinner and his 'Yellow Boys' Irregular cavalry in the wars of India between the British, Mahratta, Rajput, Mogul, Sikh & Pindarree Forces.

A CAVALRY OFFICER DURING THE SEPOY REVOLT *by A. R. D. Mackenzie*—Experiences with the 3rd Bengal Light Cavalry, the Guides and Sikh Irregular Cavalry from the outbreak to Delhi and Lucknow.

A NORFOLK SOLDIER IN THE FIRST SIKH WAR *by J W Baldwin*—Experiences of a private of H.M. 9th Regiment of Foot in the battles for the Punjab, India 1845-6.

TOMMY ATKINS' WAR STORIES: 14 FIRST HAND ACCOUNTS—Fourteen first hand accounts from the ranks of the British Army during Queen Victoria's Empire.

THE WATERLOO LETTERS *by H. T. Siborne*—Accounts of the Battle by British Officers for its Foremost Historian.

NEY: GENERAL OF CAVALRY VOLUME 1—1769-1799 *by Antoine Bulos*—The Early Career of a Marshal of the First Empire.

NEY: MARSHAL OF FRANCE VOLUME 2—1799-1805 *by Antoine Bulos*—The Early Career of a Marshal of the First Empire.

AIDE-DE-CAMP TO NAPOLEON *by Philippe-Paul de Ségur*—For anyone interested in the Napoleonic Wars this book, written by one who was intimate with the strategies and machinations of the Emperor, will be essential reading.

TWILIGHT OF EMPIRE *by Sir Thomas Ussher & Sir George Cockburn*—Two accounts of Napoleon's Journeys in Exile to Elba and St. Helena: Narrative of Events by Sir Thomas Ussher & Napoleon's Last Voyage: Extract of a diary by Sir George Cockburn.

PRIVATE WHEELER *by William Wheeler*—The letters of a soldier of the 51st Light Infantry during the Peninsular War & at Waterloo.

LEONAUR

ALSO FROM LEONAUR
AVAILABLE IN SOFTCOVER OR HARDCOVER WITH DUST JACKET

OFFICERS & GENTLEMEN *by Peter Hawker & William Graham*—Two Accounts of British Officers During the Peninsula War: Officer of Light Dragoons by Peter Hawker & Campaign in Portugal and Spain by William Graham .

THE WALCHEREN EXPEDITION *by Anonymous*—The Experiences of a British Officer of the 81st Regt. During the Campaign in the Low Countries of 1809.

LADIES OF WATERLOO *by Charlotte A. Eaton, Magdalene de Lancey & Juana Smith*—The Experiences of Three Women During the Campaign of 1815: Waterloo Days by Charlotte A. Eaton, A Week at Waterloo by Magdalene de Lancey & Juana's Story by Juana Smith.

JOURNAL OF AN OFFICER IN THE KING'S GERMAN LEGION *by John Frederick Hering*—Recollections of Campaigning During the Napoleonic Wars.

JOURNAL OF AN ARMY SURGEON IN THE PENINSULAR WAR *by Charles Boutflower*—The Recollections of a British Army Medical Man on Campaign During the Napoleonic Wars.

ON CAMPAIGN WITH MOORE AND WELLINGTON *by Anthony Hamilton*—The Experiences of a Soldier of the 43rd Regiment During the Peninsular War.

THE ROAD TO AUSTERLITZ *by R. G. Burton*—Napoleon's Campaign of 1805.

SOLDIERS OF NAPOLEON *by A. J. Doisy De Villargennes & Arthur Chuquet*—The Experiences of the Men of the French First Empire: Under the Eagles by A. J. Doisy De Villargennes & Voices of 1812 by Arthur Chuquet .

INVASION OF FRANCE, 1814 *by F. W. O. Maycock*—The Final Battles of the Napoleonic First Empire.

LEIPZIG—A CONFLICT OF TITANS *by Frederic Shoberl*—A Personal Experience of the 'Battle of the Nations' During the Napoleonic Wars, October 14th-19th, 1813.

SLASHERS *by Charles Cadell*—The Campaigns of the 28th Regiment of Foot During the Napoleonic Wars by a Serving Officer.

BATTLE IMPERIAL *by Charles William Vane*—The Campaigns in Germany & France for the Defeat of Napoleon 1813-1814.

SWIFT & BOLD *by Gibbes Rigaud*—The 60th Rifles During the Peninsula War.

AVAILABLE ONLINE AT www.leonaur.com

LEONAUR

ALSO FROM LEONAUR
AVAILABLE IN SOFTCOVER OR HARDCOVER WITH DUST JACKET

OMPTEDA OF THE KING'S GERMAN LEGION *by Christian von Ompteda*—A Hanoverian Officer on Campaign Against Napoleon.

LIEUTENANT SIMMONS OF THE 95TH (RIFLES) *by George Simmons*—Recollections of the Peninsula, South of France & Waterloo Campaigns of the Napoleonic Wars.

A HORSEMAN FOR THE EMPEROR *by Jean Baptiste Gazzola*—A Cavalryman of Napoleon's Army on Campaign Throughout the Napoleonic Wars.

SERGEANT LAWRENCE *by William Lawrence*—With the 40th Regt. of Foot in South America, the Peninsular War & at Waterloo.

CAMPAIGNS WITH THE FIELD TRAIN *by Richard D. Henegan*—Experiences of a British Officer During the Peninsula and Waterloo Campaigns of the Napoleonic Wars.

CAVALRY SURGEON *by S. D. Broughton*—On Campaign Against Napoleon in the Peninsula & South of France During the Napoleonic Wars 1812-1814.

MEN OF THE RIFLES *by Thomas Knight, Henry Curling & Jonathan Leach*—The Reminiscences of Thomas Knight of the 95th (Rifles) by Thomas Knight, Henry Curling's Anecdotes by Henry Curling & The Field Services of the Rifle Brigade from its Formation to Waterloo by Jonathan Leach.

THE ULM CAMPAIGN 1805 *by F. N. Maude*—Napoleon and the Defeat of the Austrian Army During the 'War of the Third Coalition'.

SOLDIERING WITH THE 'DIVISION' *by Thomas Garrety*—The Military Experiences of an Infantryman of the 43rd Regiment During the Napoleonic Wars.

SERGEANT MORRIS OF THE 73RD FOOT *by Thomas Morris*—The Experiences of a British Infantryman During the Napoleonic Wars-Including Campaigns in Germany and at Waterloo.

A VOICE FROM WATERLOO *by Edward Cotton*—The Personal Experiences of a British Cavalryman Who Became a Battlefield Guide and Authority on the Campaign of 1815.

NAPOLEON AND HIS MARSHALS *by J. T. Headley*—The Men of the First Empire.

LEONAUR

ALSO FROM LEONAUR
AVAILABLE IN SOFTCOVER OR HARDCOVER WITH DUST JACKET

ESCAPE FROM THE FRENCH *by Edward Boys*—A Young Royal Navy Midshipman's Adventures During the Napoleonic War.

THE VOYAGE OF H.M.S. PANDORA *by Edward Edwards R. N. & George Hamilton, edited by Basil Thomson*—In Pursuit of the Mutineers of the Bounty in the South Seas—1790-1791.

MEDUSA *by J. B. Henry Savigny and Alexander Correard and Charlotte-Adélaïde Dard* —Narrative of a Voyage to Senegal in 1816 & The Sufferings of the Picard Family After the Shipwreck of the Medusa.

THE SEA WAR OF 1812 VOLUME 1 *by A. T. Mahan*—A History of the Maritime Conflict.

THE SEA WAR OF 1812 VOLUME 2 *by A. T. Mahan*—A History of the Maritime Conflict.

WETHERELL OF H. M. S. HUSSAR *by John Wetherell*—The Recollections of an Ordinary Seaman of the Royal Navy During the Napoleonic Wars.

THE NAVAL BRIGADE IN NATAL *by C. R. N. Burne*—With the Guns of H. M. S. Terrible & H. M. S. Tartar during the Boer War 1899-1900.

THE VOYAGE OF H. M. S. BOUNTY *by William Bligh*—The True Story of an 18th Century Voyage of Exploration and Mutiny.

SHIPWRECK! *by William Gilly*—The Royal Navy's Disasters at Sea 1793-1849.

KING'S CUTTERS AND SMUGGLERS: 1700-1855 *by E. Keble Chatterton*—A unique period of maritime history-from the beginning of the eighteenth to the middle of the nineteenth century when British seamen risked all to smuggle valuable goods from wool to tea and spirits from and to the Continent.

CONFEDERATE BLOCKADE RUNNER *by John Wilkinson*—The Personal Recollections of an Officer of the Confederate Navy.

NAVAL BATTLES OF THE NAPOLEONIC WARS *by W. H. Fitchett*—Cape St. Vincent, the Nile, Cadiz, Copenhagen, Trafalgar & Others.

PRISONERS OF THE RED DESERT *by R. S. Gwatkin-Williams*—The Adventures of the Crew of the Tara During the First World War.

U-BOAT WAR 1914-1918 *by James B. Connolly/Karl von Schenk*—Two Contrasting Accounts from Both Sides of the Conflict at Sea D uring the Great War.

LEONAUR

ALSO FROM LEONAUR
AVAILABLE IN SOFTCOVER OR HARDCOVER WITH DUST JACKET

FARAWAY CAMPAIGN *by F. James*—Experiences of an Indian Army Cavalry Officer in Persia & Russia During the Great War.

REVOLT IN THE DESERT *by T. E. Lawrence*—An account of the experiences of one remarkable British officer's war from his own perspective.

MACHINE-GUN SQUADRON *by A. M. G.*—The 20th Machine Gunners from British Yeomanry Regiments in the Middle East Campaign of the First World War.

A GUNNER'S CRUSADE *by Antony Bluett*—The Campaign in the Desert, Palestine & Syria as Experienced by the Honourable Artillery Company During the Great War .

DESPATCH RIDER *by W. H. L. Watson*—The Experiences of a British Army Motorcycle Despatch Rider During the Opening Battles of the Great War in Europe.

TIGERS ALONG THE TIGRIS *by E. J. Thompson*—The Leicestershire Regiment in Mesopotamia During the First World War.

HEARTS & DRAGONS *by Charles R. M. F. Crutwell*—The 4th Royal Berkshire Regiment in France and Italy During the Great War, 1914-1918.

INFANTRY BRIGADE: 1914 *by John Ward*—The Diary of a Commander of the 15th Infantry Brigade, 5th Division, British Army, During the Retreat from Mons.

DOING OUR 'BIT' *by Ian Hay*—Two Classic Accounts of the Men of Kitchener's 'New Army' During the Great War including *The First 100,000 & All In It.*

AN EYE IN THE STORM *by Arthur Ruhl*—An American War Correspondent's Experiences of the First World War from the Western Front to Gallipoli-and Beyond.

STAND & FALL *by Joe Cassells*—With the Middlesex Regiment Against the Bolsheviks 1918-19.

RIFLEMAN MACGILL'S WAR *by Patrick MacGill*—A Soldier of the London Irish During the Great War in Europe including *The Amateur Army, The Red Horizon & The Great Push.*

WITH THE GUNS *by C. A. Rose & Hugh Dalton*—Two First Hand Accounts of British Gunners at War in Europe During World War 1- Three Years in France with the Guns and With the British Guns in Italy.

THE BUSH WAR DOCTOR *by Robert V. Dolbey*—The Experiences of a British Army Doctor During the East African Campaign of the First World War.

www.ingramcontent.com/pod-product-compliance
Lightning Source LLC
Chambersburg PA
CBHW032049080426
42733CB00006B/209